Buddha Nature

Buddha Nature

Oral Teachings by
Geshe Sonam Rinchen

Translated and edited
by
Ruth Sonam

LIBRARY OF TIBETAN WORKS & ARCHIVES

ISBN: 81-86470-34-4

Published by the Library of Tibetan Works and Archives, Dharamsala,
and printed at Indraprastha Press (CBT), 4 Bahadurshah Zafar Marg,
New Delhi – 110002

Contents

❧

Translator's Preface

There is a commonly held western view that Buddhism is profoundly pessimistic because of the Buddha's emphasis on the inevitability and ubiquity of physical and mental suffering and because of his insistence on the need to contemplate the imminence of our own death. His teaching is, therefore, erroneously regarded as fostering a rejection of life and a yearning for extinction. Nothing could be further from the truth, and the joy and vitality of many authentic practitioners are living proof of this fact.

The Buddha's teaching is, on the contrary, supremely optimistic, for he points to the hidden potential we possess, of which most of us are totally unaware. He is like a water diviner who reveals to us an inexhaustible source of pure water. This potential, variously referred to as the seed for uncontaminated mind, the disposition or as Buddha nature, is present in every living being but needs to be activated through a constellation of positive conditions. As human beings, who enjoy all kinds of good fortune and freedom from many limitations and obstacles, we are in the ideal position to create and meet with these conditions.

We are not condemned to remain as we are, helplessly governed by confusion and by our many disturbing emotions, which frequently compel us to act in destructive ways. Nor do we need to await the grace of some higher being. Through activating our inner potential or basic disposition, we can free ourselves from all faults and develop undreamed of marvellous abilities, which culminate in the attainment of enlightenment. We, too, can become Buddhas. For this enterprise we need the skilled guidance of spiritual teachers, but the ultimate responsibility lies with us because it is through our own efforts that this hidden treasure will be unearthed to make us rich beyond measure.

The Buddha lays bare the different layers of suffering we experience to make us fully acknowledge it, so that we will look for a way to rid ourselves of it. He compels us to examine the turbulent states of mind which act as a basis for this suffering, so that we can begin to uproot them. He stresses the ephemeral nature of our present good fortune and the imminence of death to give us a sense of urgency and the impetus to begin the process of awakening and fulfilling our potential now.

Western psychology is primarily concerned with describing unhealthy emotions and states of mind. Buddhist psychology also does this but goes further to delineate all those emotions and states of mind which can contribute to our transformation and full flowering. The Buddha's teaching shows us how to rid ourselves of those mental activities which act as obstacles to our development and to our own and others' well-being and how to cultivate those which are beneficial and bring true happiness.

Although at times we may feel that our negative emotions are so deeply ingrained and habitual that they seem to be an integral part of us, the Buddha's message is that these are like pollutants in water and that our mental activity can be distilled because of the clear light nature of our minds which is fundamentally good and untainted. This is indisputably a source of great hope and optimism.

Ruth Sonam
Dharamsala, 2003

Publisher's Note

❦

The Ven. Geshe Sonam Rinchen taught a course on Buddha nature during the latter part of 2000 to international students attending classes on Buddhist philosophy and practice at the Library of Tibetan Works and Archives in Dharamsala. He explained the topic in terms of the four main schools of Buddhist philosophy, drawing on Vasubandhu's *Abhidharmakośa* (*Chos mgon pa'i mdzod*) for the Vaibhashika and Sautrantika views and on Maitreya's *Mahāyānasūtrālaṃkāra* (*Tek pa chen po'i mdo sde'i rgyan*) and *Mahāyānottaratantra* (*Tek pa chen po'i rgyud bla ma*) for the Chittamatra and Madhyamika views.

It is hoped that this small book will be of special value to its readers by helping them to recognize their own hidden potential to become enlightened.

We would like to thank Linda Roman for her valuable editorial assistance.

Publication Department
Library of Tibetan Works & Archives.

July, 2003

1

Our Precious Disposition

⋘⋙

Those who practise the Buddha's Mahayana teachings have as their aim complete enlightenment. This entails accomplishing the truth body of an enlightened being,[1] which is the full flowering of our own potential, and the form bodies which are for the benefit of others. To attain these two aspects of enlightenment, we must create the two great stores of merit and insight. Love, compassion and the spirit of enlightenment[2] are the main sources for the great store of merit or positive energy which gives rise to an enlightened being's form bodies. Understanding how things exist at their most fundamental level is the principal source of the great store of insight, from which the wisdom truth body arises.

Before we can create these stores, our Mahayana disposition[3] must awaken, and this can only occur when we have become aware of its presence. Discussion of whether or not we have this precious potential makes us realize how little we actually know about ourselves.

Although the awakening of the Mahayana disposition, which occurs when we develop great compassion and great love—compassion and love which embrace all living beings without exception—necessarily precedes the development of the spirit of enlightenment, Maitreya's *Ornament for Clear Realization*[4] begins by explaining the spirit of enlightenment. This is followed by general instructions on how to attain enlightenment, after which Maitreya describes the second of the five paths, the path of preparation.[5] Only after this does he present the Mahayana disposition, whose presence makes possible the practices he then outlines.

Maitreya's *Ornament for the Mahayana Sutras* begins by arousing faith in the authenticity of the Great Vehicle and by describing what is involved in taking refuge. The main part of the text starts with an explanation of the Mahayana disposition as the basis for developing insights. With the same intention Gampopa also discusses it first in his *Ornament for Liberation*.[6] He cites the shorter *State Beyond Sorrow Sutra*[7] which states that all living beings have Buddha nature or the disposition for enlightenment. The longer *State Beyond Sorrow Sutra*[8] says that just as the potential for butter is present in all milk, so the potential for enlightenment is present in all living beings. Nevertheless, without churning the milk we will never get butter. Similarly, without activating our inherent potential we will never attain enlightenment. Because the spirit of enlightenment can be newly developed in any of the six realms of existence, it follows that it must also be possible to awaken the Mahayana disposition in these realms, which presupposes its presence in all living beings.

Though sutras, such as the *State Beyond Sorrow Sutra* mentioned above, indicate that all living beings have the potential for complete enlightenment, the lower schools of Buddhist philosophy[9] assert that there are three final vehicles,[10] and thus three corresponding types of disposition and that some living beings have no disposition for enlightenment at all. These different schools of philosophy draw our attention to increasingly subtle levels of potential which we possess.

To embark on the paths which lead to liberation and enlightenment, we must isolate our bodies from physical busyness and our minds from busy thoughts. This can only be done if we are content and have few desires. Greed is having many wishes, wanting more and wanting what is better. Of course we need basic resources, but discontentment is the inability to feel satisfied with what we have. Dissatisfaction and acquisitiveness keep our minds very busy and cause us many problems. We may live in luxury, but we will feel poor as long as we are discontent. Greed and discontent are forms of craving and are only present in the desire realm.[11] Cultivating the ability to be satisfied with what we have creates the virtue of non-attachment, which may be contaminated when it is in the mindstream of an ordinary person[12] or uncontaminated when it is associated with an exalted path of insight.

The Vaibhashika school of philosophy identifies lack of greed and contentment as the essential disposition because these states of mind are regarded as the source for the insights of an exalted being, namely one who has seen reality directly. From the Vaibhashika point of view, our craving is the root of cyclic existence, and therefore non-attachment is the antidote. Not only an obstacle to the attainment of great insights, our craving prevents us from enjoying even ordinary happiness and brings suffering in many forms. We should not neglect to consider this because it is very relevant to the way we live our lives.

In the *Sutra on the Code of Ethical Discipline*[13] this disposition of the exalted is explained in terms of four features: non-attachment to clothing, food and drink, and to dwellings. The fourth is an enthusiasm for ridding ourselves of what we need to discard and for meditation.[14] Meditation refers to the fourth noble truth, namely to cultivating true paths of insight. This enables us to accomplish the third noble truth, true cessation, which is the separation from what we must overcome.

The Buddha specified that ordained people should only possess thirteen things. He also stated that the robes of an ordained person should be made from pieces of cloth that were found in cremation grounds and from other cast-off clothing and that these should be stitched together and dyed with the cheapest dye available at that time, which was yellow. This was to prevent attachment to the robes from arising, continuing and deepening.

The first three features—simple food, clothing and dwelling places—act as an antidote to craving by preventing it from developing and being sustained. The fourth counteracts the strong wish to take a high and powerful rebirth such as that of a universal monarch. It also counteracts fear of acquiring a bad reputation or experiencing some catastrophe and the wish to die before either of these can happen. If we are taking joy in ridding ourselves of what we need to discard and in creating the causes for liberation, we will not wish for a rebirth in cyclic existence that would give us authority, prestige and power. We will also not be tempted to end our life because we need a life which is as long and healthy as possible for the attainment of insights. Turning our back on cyclic existence is a form of the clear faith of appreciation.[15]

A liking for meditation, for ridding ourselves of faults and for overcoming limitations creates the virtue of non-attachment, which acts as a main cause for the insights of an exalted being. The first three features describe the conduct that creates the prerequisite conditions and indirectly leads to these insights while the fourth describes what must actually be done and is directly responsible for those insights. Decreasing our preoccupation with food, clothing and the places where we live helps us to overcome manifest attachment to what is "mine" whereas the fourth feature helps us to uproot attachment to the "I" and "mine" completely. By practising in this way, we can make rapid progress towards liberation. The four features which have been discussed here are cultivated by practitioners of both the Lesser Vehicle and the Great Vehicle. They indicate clearly and concisely what must be done to attain liberation. Greed and discontentment distract us from doing what is necessary.

Shantideva says

> So pay this body due remuneration,
> But then be sure to make it work for you.
> But do not lavish everything
> On what will not bring perfect benefit.[16]

We should provide food and clothing for our body, as we would for a servant, with the intention of making it work for us, but we must avoid devoting too much time and energy to it. In his *Treasury of Knowledge* Vasubandhu[17] mentions four ways of nurturing the body: through food, sleep, hygiene, which includes massage and exercise, and through concentration. Another is through affection, which does not just refer to others' affection towards us but also to affection for ourselves.

Although he lived surrounded by riches, His Holiness the seventh Dalai Lama[18] was a great practitioner of non-attachment. He did not think of these things as his own, and on occasions when he had to wear special robes, he would request them from his principal attendant as if he were simply borrowing them. Here, the criterion is not how much or how little we own but to what extent we are attached to our property. There can be no doubt, however, that the more we own, the more time it takes to look after our possessions, which is very discouraging because we become their servants.

The Sautrantika school identifies the disposition as the seed or potential for uncontaminated mind,[19] namely for the realizations of an exalted being. This seed is implanted and reinforced through virtuous activities such as hearing, thinking and meditating on the teachings. There is no beginning to the time that living beings have spent in cyclic existence. No new living beings come into existence because something that does not have consciousness cannot become a conscious entity. In their different rebirths living beings experience happiness and suffering, and that happiness is the outcome of past virtue, so it can be said that no living being is entirely without virtue and thus without the seed for uncontaminated mind.

The Chittamatra school also regards the disposition as the potential for uncontaminated mind, namely for the paths of insight of exalted beings. It has been present in us naturally and continuously throughout all our rebirths. For the Chittamatra proponents of eight kinds of consciousness, it is carried by foundational consciousness. According to those who assert six kinds of consciousness, it is carried by mental consciousness.[20] Hearing, thinking and meditating activate it. Before it is awakened, it is the innately abiding disposition,[21] and afterwards it becomes the developmental disposition.

The Kadampa masters,[22] in discussing the disposition for enlightenment, drew on Maitreya's *Ornament for the Mahayana Sutras* and Asanga's *Bodhisattva Stages*.[23] Although both of these texts present the Chittamatra view of Buddha nature, this does not indicate that their authors necessarily held this view because Maitreya's *Ornament for Clear Realization* and his *Sublime Continuum* present the Prasangika view, as does Asanga's commentary on the *Sublime Continuum*.[24]

In his *Bodhisattva Stages*, Asanga reminds us that in dependence on this disposition we can attain enlightenment, provided we make effort. He says

> Bodhisattvas, depending upon and dwelling in the dispo-
> sition, have the fortune to become completely enlightened
> Buddhas, attaining unsurpassable complete enlightenment
> because they have the power to do so. For this reason the
> disposition is said to be the basis of good fortune.[25]

We are called fortunate ones because we possess this potential, and so enlightenment is possible. Without it we are unfortunate, and enlightenment is impossible.

According to the Chittamatra point of view, there are three types of disposition. These are all activated through hearing the Buddha's teachings. Because of this, the disposition is sometimes referred to as the imprint for hearing.[26] It is the seed that will grow into Buddhahood. The Mahayana disposition is activated by hearing instruction on the extensive and profound paths of the Great Vehicle. The disposition of the Hearer Vehicle is activated through hearing teachings on selflessness while that of the Solitary Realizer Vehicle is awakened by hearing teachings on the twelve links of dependent arising in forward and reverse sequence.[27] In each case the disposition eventually acts as the main cause for attaining the paths of insight of an exalted being in the respective vehicle.

If we did not have this potential, nothing could activate it no matter how much we listened to and contemplated the teachings. The fact that we have this precious disposition is a source of profound hope, but it can only yield enlightenment if we provide the necessary conditions for its maturation.

2

Understanding our Disposition

❧❀❧

The *Ornament for the Mahayana Sutras* explains the disposition for enlightenment in nine points.

> Possession, supremacy, identity
> Signs, categories of the disposition,
> Drawbacks, benefits and illustrations
> Of both—all have four features.[28]

The first is that living beings possess it. The second is that the disposition for the Great Vehicle is supreme. The third defines its identity. The fourth examines the signs of its awakening. The fifth explains its categories. The sixth, although literally meaning drawbacks or disadvantages, refers to the obstacles that prevent its awakening. The seventh explains the benefits it brings. The eighth consists of examples for the innately abiding disposition and the ninth of examples for the developmental disposition.

The first, possession, refers to the fact that living beings possess it. Because of their different inclinations they have disparate aims and interests, and therefore they will practise in different ways. This necessarily leads to different results. Maitreya's *Ornament for the Mahayana Sutras* says

> Due to propensities and aspirations,
> And division into different practices,
> Different results are envisaged. So they can
> Certainly be said to possess the disposition.[29]

Even before we embark on the paths of insight, we already have different propensities and aspirations. When we begin to cultivate these paths, our aims will vary depending on those propensities and so will the practices in which we engage. For example, those inclined to the Solitary Realizer Vehicle will accumulate more merit over a longer period than practitioners of the Hearer Vehicle, but their merit will still be less than that created by practitioners of the Great Vehicle.

We can observe something similar in secular terms when someone, for instance, is interested in medicine and has a wish to help others. If that person has the opportunity to do medical studies, he or she will probably become a successful doctor. Someone else may be interested in technology while others are artistically inclined, and if these inclinations are fostered, they will lead to fulfilment whereas this will not be the case if people are forced to go against the grain.

The second of the nine points mentioned in Maitreya's *Ornament for the Mahayana Sutras* is that the disposition for the Great Vehicle is superior to that for the Lesser Vehicle and is the supreme disposition. *The Ornament* says

> Because it is superlative virtue,
> All and very meaningful,
> Acting as cause for the inexhaustible,
> It is said to be the supreme disposition.[30]

When the Mahayana disposition is awakened, it eventually gives rise to the ten powers and four kinds of fearlessness[31] of a fully enlightened Buddha, which constitute extraordinary virtue and are radiantly pure in that they are free from the two obstructions.[32] When the disposition of the Lesser Vehicle is awakened, it does not lead to these results nor can it give rise to the ability to perceive the two truths directly and simultaneously, the mark of complete enlightenment. The awakening of the Mahayana disposition is characterized by the willingness to take responsibility for the well-being of all others while the awakened Hinayana disposition is orientated towards the accomplishment of one's personal well-being and freedom from cyclic existence. The awakened Mahayana disposition is also superior in that it is accompanied by great love, great compassion, the spirit of enlightenment and excellent dedication of all virtue created to the highest enlightenment of all living beings.

As is often said of great compassion, the Mahayana disposition is the basis for the development of all good qualities and insights. This occurs because a true practitioner of the Great Vehicle has gained the insights and understood the practices of the other two vehicles.

Otherwise it would be impossible for him or her to guide others who may be inclined towards those practices.

The disposition for the Great Vehicle is the cause for the culmination of the two great stores of merit and insight in complete enlightenment, which is supremely meaningful because of its importance and which the disposition for the Lesser Vehicle cannot yield. When enlightenment is gained, the virtue that has arisen through the presence of the Mahayana disposition does not discontinue but remains inexhaustible until all living beings, for whose sake enlightenment was attained, themselves become enlightened. This quality is likened to a tree which bears fruit year after year. In the case of the Hinayana disposition, the virtue created through it ends when one's purpose of personal liberation has been accomplished. It is, therefore, similar to a tree which dies once it has borne fruit. This indicates the vast difference made by our intention when we practise.

The third point mentioned in *The Ornament* defines the identity of the disposition. The innately abiding disposition acts as the basis or reliance, and the developmental disposition relies upon and is dependent on it. The innately abiding disposition is that which is activated through hearing, thinking and meditating. The activation occurs through the creation of virtue. This implants new potential, and certain types of that potential can eventually gives rise to the wisdom of an exalted being.

We have all kinds of virtue in our mindstreams: the kind that produces good health, longevity and success in this life. Such virtue comes to an end when its result arises. There is also virtue which leads to a good rebirth as a human or celestial being. All forms of virtue do not necessarily give rise to exalted wisdom.

The innately abiding disposition is like a cause for the developmental disposition. The two are not, however, mutually exclusive like a seed and a sprout because there can be that which is both the innately abiding disposition as well as the developmental disposition. Maitreya's *Ornament* says

> The innate and the developmental
> Are the reliance and the reliant.
> Know when they are present and absent
> And their qualities for liberation.[33]

The innately abiding disposition alone is like a cause but not a result. The developmental disposition combines both that which is a cause and a result. Both aspects of the disposition exist during the paths of learning, but neither exists at the time of the result, Buddhahood, because their potential has been fulfilled.

From the paths of accumulation and preparation—the paths on which emptiness is still experienced by way of a mental image and not directly but during which the practitioner emulates that direct experience with belief[34]—until Buddhahood, the disposition makes good qualities keep developing and growing. It has the attribute of freeing the one who possesses it from the extremes of worldly existence and solitary personal peace because through its presence good qualities continue to develop.

The fourth of the nine points mentioned by Maitreya concerns signs that indicate the awakening of our innate disposition. They mark the awakening of the Mahayana disposition. *The Ornament* says

> Before beginning—compassion,
> Belief and also patience,
> Thorough engagement in virtue.
> Know these as the signs of the disposition.[35]

The backbone of the Great Vehicle is the spirit of enlightenment, which must be preceded by the development of great compassion. The first sign of the awakening Mahayana disposition is strong compassion—a feeling that the suffering of other living beings is unbearable. Each time we cultivate love and compassion, we implant the seeds for these feelings more and more firmly, so that eventually they arise spontaneously for all those whom we encounter. It stands to reason that it must be so because the more we indulge our negative thoughts such as greed, the stronger they grow, and if we fail to curb our anger, it arises automatically in response to even quite minor provocations.

The second sign is a sense of inspiration and a surge of conviction and belief when hearing the profound and extensive teachings of the Great Vehicle. When Geshe Chekawa heard the words "May I accept defeat and offer the victory to them" from Geshe Langritangpa's *Eight Verses for Training the Mind*,[36] he felt as though he had found what had been missing from his practice and was deeply moved. The third sign is that we become better able to bear hardships for the sake of others' good, and the fourth is that we engage in our work for others and practise the six perfections[37] with joy and enthusiasm.

These signs allow us to understand that the result towards which the disposition is directed will be accomplished. Other signs are that our physical and verbal behaviour becomes more gentle, peaceful and controlled. We are sincere, free from guile and loving to others. Without bad thoughts and intentions towards them, we treat all living beings with consideration and respect. The circumstances in which we find ourselves are ideal for awakening our Mahayana disposition because we can receive the teachings of the Great Vehicle from authentic teachers and we have the aspiration to practise.

The fifth point concerns classification of the disposition. *The Ornament* says

> The disposition is determinate or indeterminate;
> It can or cannot be subverted by conditions—
> That in brief is the classification
> Of the disposition into four aspects.[38]

A classification into four is presented: the disposition may be determinate or indeterminate, and certain conditions may or may not have the power to subvert it. In general it can be said that a disposition which is determinate cannot be subverted by the presence of such conditions whereas that which is indeterminate can be affected. For instance, someone whose disposition is determinate, in that it is orientated towards the enlightenment of the Lesser Vehicle, may come across a Mahayana teacher and hear teachings on the profound and extensive paths of the Great Vehicle. He or she may for a time practise these teachings but will eventually revert to the practices of the Lesser Vehicle. Those whose disposition is indeterminate may come into contact with a Mahayana teacher, and through this encounter the Mahayana disposition may be awakened in them.

The sixth of the nine points relates to the obstructions which prevent the disposition from awakening. *The Ornament* says

> Familiarity with disturbing emotions,
> Bad friends, poverty and oppression by others—

> Know that in brief there are four
> Obstacles to the disposition.[39]

The first obstacle is the predominance of a particular disturbing emotion. It may be anger, clinging attachment or confusion. Those ruled by confusion may have particularly strong conceptions of a self and of true existence, and they may be mentally dull. We should understand, however, that we do not need to remain locked in such a condition, for we can overcome it. If we have allowed any of the disturbing emotions to arise unchecked in the past and have not regarded it as faulty, it will arise quite automatically in this life. A predominant disturbing emotion, because of our great familiarity with it, will again and again interfere with our practice and make it impossible for us to awaken our Mahayana disposition until we have counteracted it.

The second obstacle is the influence of bad friends. These may well be people who greet us with a smile and are affectionate to us. However, under their influence our disturbing emotions increase, our actions become more non-virtuous and we gradually grow distant from our spiritual teachers and the teachings. Though we should not necessarily avoid and certainly should not be hostile to people whose company affects us in this way, we must take great care not to allow their conduct and views to influence us.

The third obstacle is a lack of basic necessities. If we do not have anywhere to live, are constantly short of food and cannot afford medical treatment when we are sick, our circumstances will prevent us from awakening our Mahayana disposition because our minds will be preoccupied with getting what we need for survival.

The fourth obstacle is being in the power of others and not having sufficient control over one's own life. Some people's work situation is so precarious that they may lose their job for making the slightest mistake. Others live in constant fear under the tyranny of others. After the Chinese invasion of Tibet, Tibetans had to do all kinds of back-breaking manual labour under the most severe conditions. Then in the evenings after work, they had to attend indoctrination and struggle sessions. This left them no time or energy for much else.

The seventh point regards the benefits of awakening the Mahayana disposition. *The Ornament* says

If eventually you go to a bad rebirth,
You will quickly gain freedom. Moreover,
You will experience only minor suffering,
And, with aversion, make mature living beings.⁴⁰

Even those who have done much wrong in the past will not quickly take a bad rebirth and will in the meantime be able to create much positive energy through the awakening of their Mahayana disposition. This will gradually purify their previous wrong-doing. As a result, when they do take a bad rebirth, they will not remain there long but will soon escape from it. While they are in that rebirth, they will experience relatively little suffering. Yet it will help strengthen their aversion to cyclic existence as well as their wish for freedom, and they will do what they can to help others in the same bad rebirth to become mature. In the *Buddha Avatamsaka Sutra* Manjushri tells Subhuti that just as the fires at the end of the aeon will consume everything instantly and turn it into ash, so the spirit of enlightenment has the power to decimate the imprints left by our former wrong-doing.

The eighth point illustrates the innately abiding disposition by way of an analogy with four similarities. *The Ornament* says

Know the disposition is like a goldmine:
A source of infinite virtue,
Endowed with wisdom, stainlessness
And also a source of power.⁴¹

The innately abiding disposition is like a goldmine, for just as a goldmine is the source of much gold, all the limitless virtues and good qualities related to the paths and stages come from the innately abiding disposition. Just as the gold from the mine is bright, the innately abiding disposition gives rise to the illuminating and resplendent understanding of selflessness. The gold from the mine is unalloyed, and similarly from the disposition comes freedom from stains, a state free from the presence of disturbing emotions. The pure gold from the mine is highly malleable. Similarly the disposition allows us to develop an extremely pliant state of mind through the practice of meditative stabilization. This pliancy leads to different powers such as clairvoyance that allow us to work more effectively for the benefit of others.

The ninth point illustrates the developmental disposition. *The Ornament* says

> Know the disposition is like a trove of the best jewels
> Because it is the cause of great enlightenment,
> Of great wisdom, surpassing concentration
> And a source for the good of many living beings.[42]

A treasure trove of the best jewels contains many different kinds. They are of excellent shape, colour and size, and they are numerous. The developmental disposition of the Great Vehicle acts as a cause for highest enlightenment. It is the basis for the understanding that things are empty of true existence supported by special skilful means. It is also the basis for superlative meditative stabilization and a source of inexhaustible activity for the good of living beings.

According to the Chittamatra school do all living beings have Buddha nature? Those who see the disadvantages of cyclic existence but feel no aversion, who hear about the marvellous qualities of enlightenment and of enlightened beings but feel no faith, who have no sense of shame based on self-respect and on the wish to be a good human being, who have no sense of decency in relation to those who are generally esteemed, who see the suffering of living beings but feel no compassion and who perform only harmful actions and feel no regret, according to Asanga, lack the disposition for enlightenment. *The Ornament* says

> Some definitely do only what is mistaken;
> Some destroy all that is white;
> Some have no virtue concordant with whiteness;
> Possessing inferior whiteness, bereft of the causes.[43]

Some are involved in negative activities of which the most serious are the five gravely non-virtuous actions.[44] Some have damaged their white virtue through anger. Anger is extremely destructive because it makes us unhappy, brings us and others suffering and damages the virtue we have created. It thus deprives us of happiness, which is the normal result of virtue. Wrong views also destroy the continuity of virtue. This destruction does not happen immediately. One begins to hold a wrong view, such as the view that there is no connection between actions and their effects as described by the Buddha, but gradually the wrong view becomes more entrenched, and our virtue grows weaker. The effects are insidious.

Some have created merit which can yield good health, happiness and prosperity in this life or which can lead to a good rebirth in cyclic existence, yet they lack the merit that leads to and is therefore concordant with liberation, which here is referred to as "whiteness."

One interpretation is that in the above-mentioned three cases the developmental disposition temporarily cannot arise but the innately abiding disposition is present. For instance, those who have created serious negative actions will not be able to activate their developmental disposition until they have purified themselves of these actions. Although from the point of view of the Great Vehicle it is possible to purify all negative actions, purifying actions as grave as killing one's father or mother is not easy. Development of the spirit of enlightenment or the understanding of reality has the power to do so. Those who have created virtue but not that which is concordant with liberation can awaken their developmental disposition when they take steps to create the prerequisite kind of virtue.

According to this interpretation there is a fourth category of those who have created some merit, here referred to as inferior whiteness, but who lack the seed for uncontaminated mind and therefore have no potential for enlightenment.

Another reading of the text presents the first three categories in the same way and adds another category, namely those possessing inferior whiteness, who have created some virtue, which could potentially lead to the enlightenment of the Hearer and Solitary Realizer Vehicles, but who make no effort to develop it. In these four cases the disposition is temporarily obstructed. The words "bereft of the causes" are taken to refer to a fifth category—those who do not have any basic virtue that could act as a cause for liberation. They are said to be entirely without the disposition for enlightenment and lack the seed for uncontaminated mind.

An objection is raised that to claim some living beings are totally bereft of the disposition for enlightenment goes against the following lines in *The Ornament*:

Suchness is purely there
In all without any difference.
Therefore all living beings have
The essence of Those Gone to Bliss.[45]

This verse seems to indicate clearly that all living beings have Buddha nature. The proponents of Chittamatra tenets reply that when the *Essence of Those Thus Gone Sutra*[46] indicates that all living beings have the essence of Those Gone to Bliss, it actually means that they all have suchness as their nature. Its presence does not affect the fact that for the Chittamatrins those with no seed for uncontaminated mind have no disposition for enlightenment.

Some deny that Chittamatrins assert there are living beings without any disposition for enlightenment. In that case all beings should have the potential to attain highest enlightenment, and the Chittamatra assertion of three final vehicles would be invalid. If one argues that some lack the disposition for supreme enlightenment, one would be obliged to concede that there could be some who lack the disposition for enlightenment as a Solitary Realizer and others who lack the disposition for enlightenment as a Hearer. Thus there would necessarily be some who are entirely without any disposition at all for enlightenment.

The Mahayana disposition gives rise to very great qualities. With the wish to benefit others, Bodhisattvas teach the two truths and in association with this the extensive and profound ways in which to create the two stores of merit and insight. Even if those whom they teach cannot fully comprehend what is taught, Bodhisattvas in this way arouse others' interest in the Mahayana teachings. When they work for others, Bodhisattvas show inexhaustible patience. They do not aspire to attain the mundane states of Brahma, Indra or other worldly gods because they are still within cyclic existence, nor the supramundane state of a Hearer or Solitary Realizer Foe Destroyer but supreme enlightenment itself. Everything that has been mentioned here regarding their motivation, actual activities and the result to which they aspire is the outcome of their Mahayana disposition.

All the attributes of enlightenment such as the ten powers and so forth, the attainment of supreme joy and happiness, the ability to pacify others' suffering and the many ways of achieving one's own good and of benefiting others are the result of the disposition for enlightenment. Thus everything good during the causal stage which precedes enlightenment and the resultant state of enlightenment itself comes from this precious disposition.

The Ornament says

> It produces the spreading *bodhi* tree of great qualities,
> Enables attainment of happiness and pacification
>   of great suffering,
> Bearing the fruit of one's own and others' well-being—
> Therefore this supreme disposition is like a sound root.[47]

The disposition is the sound, healthy and firm root of a wish-fulfilling tree. From this root comes the wisdom which knows that all obstructions have been brought to an end and can never return. The tree is adorned with the strong branches of the two great accumulations. Its fragrant leaves provide shade and give relief from the heat of suffering. Its flowers and fruit bring complete satisfaction.

3

The Clear Light Nature of the Mind

The Madhyamika school draws on the *Essence of Those Thus Gone Sutra* and on Maitreya's *Sublime Continuum*, according to which the nature of our minds is not affected by the temporary stains which are present, such as the disturbing emotions. The fundamental nature, namely the emptiness of our minds with these stains, is the innately abiding disposition. Nagarjuna in his *Praise of the Sphere of Phenomena*[48] and Maitreya in his *Sublime Continuum* compare our minds to a cloudy sky, polluted water and alloyed gold. But the clouds are not an intrinsic part of the sky, nor are pollutants intrinsic to the water, and the alloys are not an integral part of the gold. The mind is not affected in its nature by these temporary stains but is clear and cognizant. This is its conventional nature. The *Sublime Continuum* says

> Like that which is precious, the sky and pure water,
> Its nature is always free of disturbing emotions.[49]

No matter how muddy and polluted the water is, those pollutants do not affect the actual nature of the water. When the water is muddy, a reflection will not appear clearly in it. Similarly, while our minds are affected by these temporary stains, nothing can appear to them very clearly. The pollutants are extraneous to the water. Just so, the mental stains are extraneous to the clear and cognizant nature of our minds. That clarity is its natural condition.

According to the Madhyamika school, the innately abiding disposition is the reality or suchness of the mind with stains,[50] namely its freedom from the so-called natural stain of true existence. Only the suchness of a mind with stains is called the innately abiding disposition and not every instance of suchness such as the emptiness of a table.

To the Madhyamikas, the Chittamatra assertion that the seed for uncontaminated mind is the innately abiding disposition, which is simply another name for the cause of the truth body of an enlightened being, is unacceptable. They say that if that were the case then because the developmental disposition is merely another name for the cause of the truth body, there would be no difference between it and the innately abiding disposition. Proponents of the Chittamatra view rebut this by contending that while the seed for uncontaminated mind has not been activated, it is the innately abiding disposition but once it has been activated through hearing and thinking about the teachings, it is the developmental disposition. Thus the two are not the same. They claim that the same fault of there being no difference between the two would apply to the Madhyamikas, who assert that the innately abiding disposition and the developmental disposition are other names for what becomes the truth body of an enlightened being.

The Madhyamikas answer that the fault does not apply to them because the innately abiding disposition is another name for the reality of the mind, which will eventually be the nature body of an enlightened being while the developmental disposition is the cause of the wisdom truth body. They argue that the seed for uncontaminated wisdom cannot be the innately abiding disposition because according to the proponents of true existence this seed is a product which comes into existence through causes and conditions. The Madhyamikas assert that the innately abiding disposition—the clear and cognizant nature of the mind—is a non-product whereas the developmental disposition is a product, so there is a fundamental difference between these two aspects of the disposition.

The presentation of Buddha nature according to Maitreya's *Sublime Continuum* consists of a concise explanation of the topic, its elaboration and the reasons for explaining Buddha nature. The *Sublime Continuum* presents seven topics or sources of the adamantine.[51] Sources here refer to the collection of syllables, composing words and phrases that act as a source or basis for the elucidation, revelation and understanding of the seven adamantine topics.

They are said to be adamantine because they are impenetrable and cannot be understood exactly as they are by an understanding derived from hearing and thinking about them. Words cannot fully express them. Nor can conceptual thought completely comprehend them in the way that they are experienced during the meditative equipoise of an exalted one directly perceiving their emptiness or as they are understood by such a one in the period which follows that meditative equipoise.

The first three are the three objects of refuge: the jewel of the Buddhas, the jewel of the teachings and the jewel of the spiritual community. The fourth topic is the constituent,[52] which here refers to Buddha nature; the fifth is enlightenment; the sixth is qualities, and the seventh is enlightened activity.[53] The first three are the result which is only possible through the presence of Buddha nature, the disposition for enlightenment.

The *Sublime Continuum* mentions what is said in the *Essence of Those Thus Gone Sutra*, namely that all embodied beings have the essence of Those Thus Gone, which is to say that they always have Buddha nature. The *Sublime Continuum* says

> Because the fully enlightened body emanates,
> And because suchness is undifferentiated,
> And because they have the disposition, all the embodied
> Always have the essence of Buddhahood.[54]

The three ways in which they have the essence of Those Thus Gone, also referred to as the constituent essence of Those Gone to Bliss,[55] are that they share receptivity to enlightened activity, that they have the same fundamental nature and that the disposition is present in them. The first is their receptivity to the enlightened activity which emanates from the truth body. The enlightened activity here refers to virtue. There is no living being who has never created any virtue. To create virtue one must have the potential to do so. This potential is the disposition, the essence of Those Gone to Bliss. All living beings have at some time been born as human or celestial beings, so they have been receptive to the enlightened activity which is a cause for high status, namely the happiness experienced in a good rebirth. They also have the potential to receive the enlightened activity which leads to liberation or enlightenment, states referred to as definite goodness.[56]

The second way in which all living beings have the disposition or Buddha nature is as follows: the fundamental nature or reality of the minds of ordinary beings cannot be differentiated from the fundamental nature of an enlightened being's mind. The reality of the mind with stains is the constituent which is the essence of Those Gone to Bliss. When it is the fundamental nature of the unstained mind of a Buddha, it is the nature body. Here the disposition is considered from the point of view of its nature. Of course, it is possible to differentiate between our minds and the mind of an enlightened being but not from the point of view of their fundamental nature.

The conventional nature of the mind is its clarity and cognizance. The stains are not an integral part even of the mind's conventional nature. Is there a difference between saying that the mind is not affected by stains and claiming that the nature of the mind is not affected by stains? At present our minds are definitely affected by stains, namely by the disturbing emotions and their imprints. However, if the nature of our minds were affected by these stains, we would never be able to get rid of them by applying their antidotes. For instance, if anger were integral to the mind's nature, we could never hope to become more patient. And further, if anger were a part of our minds, we would be getting rid of our minds at the same time that we rid ourselves of anger.

The disturbing attitudes and emotions along with their imprints prevent us from seeing both the clear light conventional and ultimate nature of our minds. Exalted beings see the reality of the mind in meditative equipoise, but during the subsequent period the ultimate clear light nature of the mind is again obscured. This continues to be so until one attains enlightenment. The conventional clear light nature of the mind, namely its clarity and cognizant nature, is seen by exalted beings in the period subsequent to meditative equipoise on the ultimate clear light nature of the mind. This conventional clear light nature of the mind can be perceived when the flow of thoughts which hides it is interrupted and discursive thought dies down. Even this state is difficult to achieve.

The third way in which all living beings have the essence of Those Gone to Bliss is that the disposition is present in all of them. Their innately abiding disposition eventually becomes the nature body of an enlightened being and their developmental disposition, the seed for uncontaminated mind, becomes the bodies of an enlightened being, which are products, namely their wisdom truth body, their enjoyment body and their emanation body.

When we refer to the innately abiding disposition, we are emphasizing the potential living beings have for enlightenment. When we speak about the reality of the mind with stains, we are referring to the same thing but describing its nature. This presentation of the essence of Those Gone to Bliss indicates to us that we have the complete potential for attaining the truth and form bodies of a fully enlightened being.

Some Tibetan commentators have said that both the mind's reality and its clear and cognizant nature constitute the innately abiding disposition and that the reality of the mind with stains becomes the nature body of an enlightened being while the clear and cognizant nature becomes the wisdom truth body. Vimuktisena in his *Illumination of the Twenty Thousand*,[57] which is a commentary on the *Perfection of Wisdom Sutra in Twenty-five Thousand Verses* and Maitreya's *Ornament for Clear Realization*, explicitly states that only the suchness of the mind with stains is the innately abiding disposition which becomes the nature body of an enlightened being.

If the mind's clarity and cognizance were also the innately abiding disposition, this would conflict with the Madhyamika refutation of the Chittamatrin assertion that the innately abiding disposition is the seed of uncontaminated mind and that it and the developmental dispositions are both products. The Madhyamika refutation was based on the fact that there would be no difference between the two. If the clear and cognizant nature of the mind were also the innately abiding disposition, it would, when freed from temporary stains, become the nature body of an enlightened being, which would then necessarily be a product. But the nature body is not a product—something produced as a result of causes and conditions.

In the *Sublime Continuum* there are ten points which directly indicate the clear light nature of our minds and indirectly demonstrate that the stains are temporary. These ten are followed by nine examples illustrating nine points that directly show the temporary nature of our mental obstructions and indirectly indicate the clear light nature of our minds. In fact these two emphasize the same point through affirming different aspects. The ten points in brief are

Identity, causes, effect, function, possession,
Engagement, phases, pervasion, immutability,
And lack of distinction—these are said to be
What is meant by the ultimate sphere.[58]

The ultimate sphere is the essence of Those Thus Gone. Establishing the clear light nature of the mind, which here refers particularly to its lack of inherent existence, is of supreme importance. The most fundamental of the stains[59] is the conception of inherent existence, which is a distorted perception. If the mind were not empty of inherent existence, then the conception of inherent existence would not be a wrong cognition[60] but would be a perception in accordance with fact and therefore could never be and would not need to be removed.

This explanation of the mind's clear light nature is based upon a sutra passage saying, "Monks, the mind is not a mind [which is inherently existent]. The nature of the mind is clear light."[61]

The first of the points, identity,[62] concerns the identification of the clear light nature of the mind in terms of the three points mentioned earlier, namely that all beings possess the potential to receive the enlightened activity of the wisdom truth body, which is compared to a jewel of great power that can fulfill all wishes. All beings have the potential to attain the wisdom truth body themselves.

There is no difference between the suchness of the mind with stains and the suchness of an enlightened being's mind. Just as space, wherever it is, is a mere absence of obstruction, the suchness of the mind is its mere absence of inherent existence.

All living beings have the disposition for enlightenment. The innately abiding disposition and the developmental disposition eventually become the nature and other bodies of an enlightened being. The developmental disposition is the seed of uncontaminated mind and holds the moisture of compassion for all living beings, through which the seed will germinate and produce its seedling.

We cannot point to any living being and say we have never felt compassion for this one because they all, at one time or another, have been in very close relationships with us as our fathers, mothers, partners, siblings and children, and at those times we have had compassion for them. They, too, have all had compassion for us. This means we have the potential for compassion but not that we already have the great compassion which embraces all beings. Our anger at present makes this impossible, and we are not yet equipped with strong enough antidotes to combat it. However, that potential will eventually act as the main cause for the development of great compassion.

Even when we have developed compassion that extends to all living beings, the seed for uncontaminated states of mind is still present and active because our compassion has not yet reached perfection and will only do so when we attain enlightenment. Love, compassion, the imprints created by hearing, thinking and meditating and the mind with stains itself are all examples of the developmental disposition. Its emptiness of intrinsic existence is the innately abiding disposition.

The second of the ten points, causes,[63] here refers to the causes for purifying the suchness of its stains and for the development of the disposition to the highest perfection, the truth body.[64] They are belief, uncontaminated wisdom, meditative stabilization and great compassion.

The suchness of our minds is always present but hidden from us by the stains, and we can only see it when these stains have been removed. We therefore speak of suchness with stains.[65] This is compared to an eye with faulty vision which does not see a distant but clearly visible object. The fault does not lie with the object but with the eye. An objection might be raised that the stains prevent us from seeing the truth body and that one could by the same logic call it the truth body with stains. However, this is not so because the stains that prevent its perception are not in the continuum of the one who possesses the truth body. If the mind did not have a clear light nature and if the stains were an integral part of it, the mind could never be purified of them just as coal, no matter how long one washes it, will never become white.

The faith of aspiration which comes from belief in or strong admiration for the Mahayana teachings is likened to a seed that leads to the development of the spirit of enlightenment. A Bodhisattva's training in uncontaminated wisdom, specifically the understanding of the fundamental nature of things, is compared to a mother because it gives birth to the Foe Destroyers of the three vehicles. The training in meditative stabilization is likened to the mother's womb. Just as the womb holds the child in a stable environment, concentration creates mental stability. Great compassion is compared to a wet nurse who suckles and nurtures the child. In his *Supplement to the Middle Way*, Chandrakirti[66] lays emphasis on its importance at the beginning, intermediately and at the end:

> Compassion alone is seen as the seed
> Of a Victor's rich harvest,
> As water for its growth, and as its ripening
> Into a source of usefulness.
> And so, first, I pay homage to compassion.

The causes mentioned, such as belief, do not produce the disposition or Buddha nature, but they purify the mental stains and enable the flowering of our Buddha nature. Without the initial fervent belief in the teachings of the Great Vehicle, it is impossible to develop great compassion or the combination of calm abiding and special insight which is unique to that vehicle.

The third of these points, the effect,[67] refers to the fact that the result of this purification and development is the truth body of an enlightened one. The *Sublime Continuum* only mentions three bodies of a Buddha—the truth body and the two form bodies. The truth body is utterly beyond all misperceptions that what is unclean is clean, what is painful is pleasurable, what is impermanent is permanent and what is empty of a self has a self.[68] The first noble truth, true suffering has four features: impermanence, painfulness, uncleanness and selflessness. Understanding these features enables one to overcome the misperceptions.

The truth body of Those Thus Gone or *tathagatas* is perfect purity because it is free from the natural stains of true existence and because all the imprints of the disturbing attitudes and emotions have been eliminated and brought to an end. It is a perfect excellent self because the non-existence of a self of persons, as attributed by non-Buddhists, and the lack of true existence of that selflessness have been understood directly in a way that pacifies all elaborations of duality, namely appearances of true existence, and prevents them from ever recurring.

The truth body of an enlightened one is perfect bliss. At present our bodies are the result of contaminated actions underlain by the disturbing emotions. Much more subtle than this is the mental body of an exalted one, the result of both non-deluded ignorance—meaning the subtle traces of ignorance, which remain and act as obstructions to knowledge of all phenomena—and uncontaminated actions motivated by these imprints of ignorance. The truth body of Those Thus Gone transcends even this mental body and is therefore perfected well-being and bliss. It is perfect permanence in the sense of total stability because of the ultimate understanding that both cyclic existence and nirvana are empty of inherent existence and because of ultimate freedom from the extremes of worldly existence and personal peace.

The misperceptions that what is unclean is clean, what is painful is pleasurable, what is impermanent is permanent and what is empty of a self has a self are distortions with regard to the conventional nature of things. To get rid of them we need to understand well the four features of the first noble truth, which are diametrically opposed to these misconceptions. Recognizing the body's impermanence, its disintegrating nature and how it is governed by other factors helps us to overcome the idea that the body is clean. Understanding its painful nature counteracts our sense of the body as a source of pleasure. Understanding emptiness is an antidote to conceptions of the self as a permanent, partless, independent entity while recognizing its selflessness is an antidote to the conception of the self as a substantially existent self-sufficient entity. In this context misconception in relation to the ultimate consists of thinking that impermanence, painfulness, uncleanness and selflessness have true existence. The selflessness referred to here is a coarse level. When subtle selflessness has been understood, there is no danger that it could be construed as truly existent.

The four factors of belief, wisdom, meditative stabilization and great compassion, mentioned in the context of the second of the ten points, also act as opponents to these misperceptions. A strong belief in the Mahayana teachings counters any dislike for them and a liking for the unclean nature of cyclic existence and thus leads to perfect purity. Wisdom understanding the nature of reality counters attachment to diverse wrong views of the self and leads to the perfected excellent self of the truth body as mentioned above. Meditative stabilization leads to perfect bliss derived from total concentration. Great compassion leads to perfect permanence because through extensive familiarity with compassion there is an uninterrupted constant flow of it for all living beings.

4

The Reality of the Mind

⊕

After identifying the clear light nature of the mind, indicating the causes that purify the mental stains which obscure it, and after showing the results of this purification, Maitreya's *Sublime Continuum* introduces the fourth point, function.[69] Those who have created the white virtue that accords with liberation think about the general and specific disadvantages of all states within cyclic existence, and realizing that suffering is an integral part of cyclic existence, they feel a revulsion towards it. Seeing the beneficial nature of the happiness associated with nirvana, they aspire to attain it. When they hear about these drawbacks and benefits or about emptiness, they get goose pimples. The ability to react in this way and to feel such aversion and aspiration indicates the presence of the disposition for liberation and the activity of Buddha nature. These feelings could not occur unless the mind had clear light nature.

The fifth of the points, possession,[70] refers to the qualities mentioned in relation to the second point, the cause, which remove the stains and develop the disposition for enlightenment, as well as to the qualities pertaining to the effect, namely the six kinds of super-knowledge and the end of contamination. The six kinds of super-knowledge mentioned here are the ability to perform miraculous feats, the divine ear, knowledge of others' minds, remembrance of past places, knowledge of death and rebirth and knowledge of the end of contamination.[71] These abilities can all be developed because of the clear light nature of the mind.

The first five kinds of super-knowledge are compared to the light coming from the flame of a butterlamp. They bring one closer to overcoming the darkness which hides the object—reality. Here the stainless exalted knowledge of the end of contamination[72] refers to direct perception that the obstructions to liberation have come to an end. It is compared to the heat that arises as fire consumes its fuel. This knowledge is possessed by Hearer and Solitary Realizer Foe

Destroyers, by Bodhisattvas on the eighth, ninth and tenth stages and by exalted Buddhas.

The end of contamination, also referred to as stainless elimination,[73] marks the end of the disturbing attitudes and emotions as well as their seeds and in particular all misconceptions of the person and aggregates as truly existent. The end of all contamination is not only stainless because these misconceptions and all other obstructions formed by the disturbing attitudes and emotions and their seeds have been eliminated, but it is also completely pure because the obstructions to knowledge of all phenomena constituted by the imprints of the disturbing emotions and appearances of true existence have also been overcome. This stainless and pure elimination is reality, whose nature is clear light with separation from the two kinds of stains or obstructions. It is compared to the bright colour of the butterlamp's flame which dispels all darkness completely. None of the obstructions are an integral part of the mind, and therefore the end of contamination is also clear light. An enlightened being remains in a state of complete illumination with constant perception of emptiness.

The ocean is an aggregation of all manner of things, such as water and caskets of jewels. Our Buddha nature is like the ocean and fervent belief in the teachings of the Great Vehicle is like a casket containing the jewels of calm abiding and special insight in a form unique to the Great Vehicle. The great compassion of a Bodhisattva which acts as a cause for the perfected compassion of an enlightened one is like the water in the ocean.

The sixth point, engagement,[74] refers to distinctions made not with regard to suchness but with regard to the basis and the degree to which the stains have or have not been removed. It refers to the progressive development as one engages with different levels of practice and gains realizations. The different kinds of basis here refer to ordinary beings, exalted beings other than Buddhas and exalted Buddhas. The suchness of their minds is the same in all three cases, and differences are not posited from the point of view of its identity. However, there are differences regarding separation from stains in relation to that suchness. Where ordinary beings are concerned, the stains have not been purified. In the case of the exalted who are not yet Buddhas, separation from one aspect of the stains has been accomplished. This refers to the intellectually formed objects eliminated by the path of seeing. Finally in the case of exalted Buddhas, complete separation from all stains or obstructions has been achieved.[75] Seeing this difference, the enlightened ones have said the suchness of living beings, in contrast to that of Buddhas, is with stains. It is a differentiation made with regard to suchness and not with regard to the disposition as Buddhas no longer have the disposition because it has been fully realized. This progressive purification can take place because of the clear light quality of the mind.

To say "suchness with stains" may sound strange to us. Our minds are affected by the disturbing emotions, which are secondary mental events of one nature with the mental consciousness that they accompany. It is possible to focus on the mind which is affected by these disturbing emotions. Were it not for them, we would be able to perceive directly our minds' emptiness of inherent existence, but these stains obscure our perception and prevent it. Suchness, the fundamental nature of our minds, is one entity with the mind itself, and both the mind and its fundamental nature are obscured by these stains. While it is possible to focus on the suchness of the mind when it is affected by the disturbing emotions, the disturbing emotions themselves, which are also awareness, cannot focus on suchness. A mind focussing on emptiness with the aspiration to understand it is a virtuous state of mind and not one governed by disturbing emotions.

The suchness of the mind with stains—its emptiness of the natural stain of true existence—is what allows living beings to gain the complete enlightenment of a Victorious One because if we take this as the focal object of our meditation, it acts as a source of all the qualities of enlightenment.

The seventh point, phases,[76] indicates that, although suchness remains the same, we go through different phases in the process of mental purification. Where the disposition of those who are still ordinary beings is concerned, there has been no purification of obstructions. The disposition of those who are exalted Bodhisattvas or exalted beings of the Hearer and Solitary Realizer vehicles but who are not yet enlightened is partly purified of obstructions. Those Thus Gone are utterly purified of all obstructions. The identity of the mind's suchness, however, is the same in each case.

In the first two cases, it is incorrect to say that ordinary living beings are an exemplification of what is not at all purified and exalted beings of what is partially purified because it is ultimate truth, the suchness of the mind, that is discussed here, so it is the suchness of their minds alone which is unpurified or partially purified. However, it can be said that Those Thus Gone exemplify that which is completely purified because the term One Thus Gone can be used not only for the person but for the truth body and the other bodies of an enlightened being as well.

In this case suchness qualified in these three ways is the basis of attribution for the three persons. Normally the person is attributed to the collection and continuum of the aggregates, but these are not the person. Similarly these three states of suchness—with no purification whatsoever, with partial purification and with complete purification of obstructions—are not the ordinary living being, the exalted one or the One Thus Gone.

The eighth point, pervasion,[77] indicates that there is movement and progression through these different phases, during which suchness is pervasive and always present. If the identity of suchness changed, it could not be present in the same form during all three phases. Three pots—one made of clay, the next of copper and the third of gold—can be classified in terms of their preciousness, but the empty space in each of them is of the same nature and is a mere absence of obstructing form. Similarly, the mere absence of inherent existence is present in all phenomena, and we should not imagine that emptiness has different aspects like blue and yellow. It is always present as the mind's nature and is undifferentiated. Differences are posited in relation to the bases of emptiness.

The ninth point, immutability,[78] indicates that throughout this progression the identity of suchness remains immutable. As has been said, the emptiness of an ordinary being's mind is no different in nature from that of an exalted being or of One Thus Gone. When enlightenment is attained, no change has taken place in the nature of the mind's emptiness, and so it is referred to as immutable reality.

One might question this point because the reality of the minds of ordinary beings and of exalted beings other than Buddhas is called reality with flaws while that of an enlightened being is referred to as reality with the quality of being free from flaws. This distinction, however, poses no problem because the mind has these flaws in a temporary way, which means they can be eliminated. It also has the potential for developing all the qualities of enlightenment. The focal object for developing these marvellous qualities is the very nature that the mind possesses. Neither the flaws nor good qualities in any way affect or change the mind's fundamental nature, its emptiness of inherent existence. Just as the ocean everywhere has the same taste, all phenomena, where their fundamental nature is concerned, have the same taste because ultimate truth will never be anything but the emptiness of inherent existence.

Different aspects of emptiness do not appear to the meditative equipoise of an exalted being. Space is present throughout the physical world. It is a mere absence of obstruction and a non-product which, because of its subtle nature, cannot be apprehended by sense perception. Its nature is unaffected by the polluting particles of the environmental world. Similarly the disposition, which is natural purity and uncontaminated, is present in all living beings and is not affected by actions or by disturbing attitudes and emotions.

The tenth point, no differentiation,[79] refers to the fact that at the time of total purification the qualities pertaining to complete liberation in the form of non-abiding nirvana are not discrete entities. The brightness of the sun, the emanation of its light and the purity of its orb are not different entities. Similarly, with complete clarity ultimate understanding directly sees things as they are, namely their fundamental nature. Exalted wisdom also extends to all phenomena, directly perceiving their diversity. Moreover there is total purity because all stains without exception have been eliminated. These three features are not different entities but qualities of the truth body with which they are one entity.

In the mind of an enlightened being, the wisdom of meditative equipoise and the wisdom subsequent to meditative equipoise are not different entities. The awareness which sees the fundamental nature of things also sees their multiplicity and vice versa. In the ultimate state beyond sorrow—non-abiding nirvana—there is every kind of good quality excluding none, and these qualities are innumerable. All the qualities of realization, whose powers are inconceivable, and the many qualities pertaining to the elimination of all stains and their imprints are not different entities.

The entity of suchness is seen to be the same no matter what phenomena are regarded, whether pure or impure, good or bad. Also all three kinds of enlightenment comprise equal freedom from the disturbing emotions. The freedom of a fully enlightened being comprises the enlightenment of a Hearer and Solitary Realizer.

These ten points are discussed to emphasize that the clear light nature of the mind is not affected by stains. Otherwise it would be impossible to purify it. For this reason the nature of the mind is like unalloyed gold, like a cloudless sky and like unpolluted water.

When a world system comes into being, it does so within space which is the mere negation or absence of tangible obstruction. First there is wind and from the movement of this wind in space comes water. Then earth forms, and the four continents as well as the supreme core mountain appear. When the life-span of a world system comes to an end, it disintegrates through fire, wind or water. The nature of space, however, is unaffected both by the world system's evolution and by its atrophy or disintegration.

Through the movement of the wind, many changes are brought about as the physical environment and the living beings within it come into existence, but these changes are temporary. Similarly the mind's fundamental nature is clear light and is a mere negation of true existence. An incorrect mental approach arises in this clear light mind just as the wind arises in space. This incorrect mental approach, which distorts how we see things, leads to the disturbing emotions from which come karmic actions. The actions are the main cause for the formation of the aggregates of this life while the disturbing emotions are the contributing conditions. Just as the seed is the main cause for the plant but requires contributing conditions such as moisture and a growing medium to germinate, so the imprints left by our actions will only lead to rebirth in cyclic existence if craving and grasping are present. Our life is brought to an end by aging, sickness and death. The clear light nature of the mind is unaffected by the whole process.

In this analogy the actions and disturbing emotions are like the water element, which acts as a basis for the earth element. The earth element represents the resultant aggregates, sources and constituents. The water element depends upon the wind element symbolized by the unstable and incorrect mental approach. The wind element depends upon space, which represents the mind's fundamental nature and ultimate truth, emptiness. This fundamental nature does not exist in the way that the incorrect mental approach apprehends things, for its nature is the object only of a mental approach that accords with fact.

While we remain uncertain about all this, we are vulnerable and easily swayed by others' opinions. When we become certain that we have Buddha nature, nothing others can say to the contrary will affect our conviction, so it is worth giving thought to these matters in depth until we gain certainty.

5

Uncovering our Hidden Treasure

❦

The previously explained ten points showing the clear light nature of the mind demonstrate that it is possible to free the mind from mental stains. The eighteen analogies and their meanings as described in Maitreya's *Sublime Continuum* emphasize that the stains are not an integral part of our minds. These analogies explain that which conceals and what is concealed and demonstrate that it is possible to attain the nature body of a Buddha free from the two kinds of obstructions.

Nine of the analogies and what they illustrate are associated with the afflicted side, and the other nine and what they signify are associated with the purified side. Those associated with the afflicted side are as follows: (1) an ugly lotus: latent desire; (2) a swarm of bees: latent anger; (3) the husk: latent ignorance; (4) a heap of filth: the three poisonous emotions manifesting strongly; (5) earth: the stage of the imprints of ignorance;[80] (6) the seed: objects to be eliminated by the path of seeing; (7) rags: objects to be eliminated by the path of meditation; (8) the womb: objects to be eliminated on the seven impure Bodhisattva stages; (9) a mould: objects to be eliminated on the eighth, ninth and tenth Bodhisattva stages.

The following nine are something precious which is hidden: (10) a Buddha: the truth body of realization; (11) honey: the truth body of teachings on the ultimate, namely on things as they are; (12) rice: the truth body of teachings on the conventional, namely on the multiplicity of things; (13) gold: suchness; (14) a treasure: the innately abiding disposition; (15) a tree: the developmental disposition; (16) a precious statue: the potential for the truth body; (17) a future universal monarch: the potential for the enjoyment body; (18) a statue: the potential for the emanation body.

Those Gone to Bliss have seen the disposition for enlightenment in all living beings, even those in the lowest hell, and for that reason have taught us how to remove the disturbing attitudes and emotions and everything which conceals this disposition. When these factors have been removed, it will become the truth body.

In the analogies that which conceals and what is concealed are all different. Regarding what these analogies illustrate, the concealing factors, such as latent desire and so forth, are in each case different but what they conceal is the essence of Those Gone to Bliss, which can be subsumed as the truth body, suchness and the disposition. All the concealing factors hide these three.

The truth body reaches living beings through enlightened activity, which they all have the potential to receive. The main way in which this happens is in the form of teachings. The first three analogies for what is hidden—a Buddha, honey and rice—illustrate that Buddha nature is the potential to receive the enlightened activity of the truth body.

The ugly, misshapen lotus symbolizes latent desire. Latent desire becomes manifest, and when it first arises, we feel joyful, but soon there is pain. One who has the clear divine eye[81] can see hidden within the ugly lotus the form of a Buddha adorned with the thirty-two major and eighty minor signs of enlightenment. When the petals are removed, this form is revealed. It symbolizes the truth body, which only the form of an enlightened one can represent in this world.

The sphere of phenomena is pure by nature of all stains of true existence. In the state of enlightenment, there is also complete purity or absence of all temporary stains. An enlightened being never again arises from the state of directly perceiving the sphere of phenomena possessing these two kinds of purity. This direct perception of an enlightened being is called the truth body of realization.[82] It is not accessible to those who are not enlightened. For this reason Buddhas manifest different form bodies: an enjoyment body for those who are already exalted beings and for others an emanation body, which is the source of the scriptures. These form bodies are not coarse as our own.

Hundreds of bees, representing anger, surround the honey. Whoever wants to get at the honey must first remove the swarm of bees. The Great Sage, the enlightened one, saw that this honey-like Buddha nature, the innately abiding disposition, is present in all living beings and when freed from stains, it becomes the nature body of an enlightened being. For this reason there are the wisdom truth body's teachings on emptiness, the ultimate. The scriptures are the effect which accords with the cause, namely an enlightened one's direct perception of the reality of his or her mind. These scriptures consist of both definitive sutras or discourses which explain the ultimate and interpretable discourses which explain the conventional.[83] When emptiness is perceived directly, it always produces bliss of the same taste just as honey is always sweet.

The husk denotes ignorance and the grain within, the wisdom truth body's teachings on conventional reality. Just as conventional reality is manifold, so too are the teachings on it. This is represented by the many forms of grain, each with a husk. If we want to cook the grain to make a meal, we must first husk it. .

The rotting heap of filth signifies the disturbing emotions when they are strongly active. We dislike touching filth and find it disgusting. The disturbing emotions produce disgusting actions that are like filth and that keep us mired in cyclic existence. If the disturbing emotions did not exist in latent form, they could not manifest in this way. The actions they produce shackle us to the three realms of cyclic existence. Those that come from anger are always non-virtuous and lead to bad rebirths.

Actions occasioned by desire and attachment or ignorance may constitute contaminated virtue and can lead to rebirth in the form and formless realms. For instance, attachment to the pleasure experienced during meditative stabilization or to the blissful peace of absorption may lead to a rebirth in the form and formless realms. However, these are undesirable rebirths because while enjoying that bliss, one creates no new merit and when previous merit is exhausted, one must once more take birth in a lower state of existence. This kind of attachment is afflicted but unspecified and not non-virtuous because non-virtue will never lead to such a rebirth. Unspecified here means it is not indicated in the scriptures as virtuous or non-virtuous, yet it is afflicted because attachment is a disturbing emotion even if not strongly active within the peaceful states of absorption of the upper realms.

A celestial being flying in the sky through clairvoyant powers sees a beautiful piece of gold jewellery that once belonged to a human.

It fell to the ground many years before, and though it is covered by layers of dirt, the gold has remained unaltered. If the celestial being points out to a human where the golden object lies, that human being will be able to uncover it. Similarly the enlightened ones see the suchness of our minds, our innately abiding disposition, which is covered by the filth of our disturbing emotions. It is there, unaltered, just like the piece of precious jewellery caked in dirt. They send a shower of the ambrosial teachings to wash away the filth.

Just as the gold remains unchanged and is not stained by the surrounding dirt but can bring happiness if worn and riches if sold, so the suchness of our minds never changes, nor is it affected by our emotions. It can lead us to lasting happiness. Through understanding the suchness of our minds and then familiarizing ourselves with it, we will attain the nature body of a Buddha.

These first four analogies for that which conceals are mainly about the disturbing emotions as they manifest in ordinary people, and they primarily stress the noxious and obstructive nature of these disturbing emotions. If we can get rid of them, everything else will come right. It is the task of an enlightened being to show us how to do it, but we must put what is taught into practice in order to experience the results.

In the first four analogies for that which is concealed, the Buddha, the honey and the rice represent the truth body while the gold represents suchness. The fifth analogy is of earth which hides a treasure. This is not a treasure of artefacts which has been buried but ore or precious stones which are naturally present in the ground. A beggar's hovel is built on this patch of land, which hides an inexhaustible treasure. The beggar knows nothing of the treasure's presence, and the treasure does not announce itself. The earth represents the stage of the imprints of ignorance. If a clairvoyant sees the treasure underground and tells the beggar, he can uncover it and be free from poverty, but until that time he will remain poor. The naturally present treasure represents our innately abiding disposition, which is a source of many good qualities. In this, it is as a treasure which, when mined, yields much gold or many jewels.

We suffer from a poverty of good qualities, such as the seven riches possessed by the exalted ones.[84] Through the Buddha's teaching on the two aspects of selflessness, we will come to see the fundamental nature of things directly and will possess the qualities of the exalted. This will enable us to gain freedom from cyclic existence. We should consider what we can learn from these examples.

The sixth example of the seed, which contains the potential for a fully grown tree laden with fruit, demonstrates how our disposition for enlightenment can become the nature body of a Buddha. By creating virtue we will eventually remove the stains and become a King of Subduers, a fully enlightened Buddha. Just as the seed germinates when the right conditions of moisture, a fertile growing medium and the conducive temperature are present, similarly our developmental disposition is activated through hearing, thinking and meditating. When supported by the spirit of enlightenment, it will bear the fruit of Buddhahood. The seed represents everything that is eliminated by the Hinayana path of seeing.

Those Thus Gone see the disposition for enlightenment even in the most humble living creatures and teach us how to remove the stains. If we practise, this precious potential will yield its fruit. In the seventh example, a golden statue wrapped in rags lies by the road, and everyone walks past it without even realizing it is there. A celestial being with clairvoyant powers sees it within the rags and alerts one of the passers-by to its presence. The rags represent everything that is eliminated by the Hinayana path of meditation. The statue made of something precious denotes the nature body. The precious material is not an artificial alloy that has been manufactured by combining various materials involving numerous causes and conditions. It is a natural material of great value. Similarly, the nature body is not constructed by causes and conditions. Through its presence the wishes of living beings can be fulfilled spontaneously. This analogy can also be taken as a statue that has appeared of its own accord in the precious material. The statue has not come into being through coarse causes and conditions such as the work of an artisan but has come into being naturally.

The enlightened ones see the precious disposition in impure living beings, concealed within all the mental defilements, and know that when these temporary defilements are removed enlightenment will follow. When we accomplish the nature body of enlightenment, we become the true protectors of others.

In the eighth example, a destitute and ugly young woman carries in her womb a future universal monarch. At present she suffers and thinks of her pregnancy as a calamity, not knowing that through the child in her womb she will attain status and power and that he will become her protector. The universal monarch symbolizes the enjoyment body. Just as a universal monarch enjoys power over several continents, the enjoyment body has dominion over and makes use of all the teachings of the Great Vehicle. The destitute woman represents everything that is eliminated on the seven impure Bodhisattva stages.

Buddhas see the clear light nature of our disposition and know that it is a source of preciousness. When the temporary stains have been removed, we will become exalted Buddhas. The clay mould hides the golden statue within it. The mould symbolizes everything that is eliminated on the pure Bodhisattva stages. The statue represents the emanation body of an enlightened being. It is made of gold, which can be turned into many different things. The emanation body's nature is exalted wisdom, which takes whatever forms will be of benefit to living beings.

Earlier when describing the mind's suchness, we said that it remains unchanged whatever the circumstances, that it is unaffected by mental stains and is a source of prosperity. We may wonder how the suchness of the mind or the innately abiding disposition, which is after all just the non-affirming negation of true existence, can be a source of great qualities and happiness. When we focus our minds on emptiness, we create virtue and a store of insight. Virtue leads to happiness, and the store of insight along with the store of merit are the causes of enlightenment.

Reference to suchness of the mind with stains emphasizes the identity of that emptiness while mention of the innately abiding disposition emphasizes its function. Because emptiness is a non-product, in that it is not produced by causes and conditions and does not produce anything else, the causal aspect here refers to the fact that emptiness is like a substratum and like space within which everything arises. It does not cause those things but allows them to come into being and to operate.

The concealing factors may be examined in greater detail. A lotus grows from the mud at the bottom of the pond. When it first opens, it is beautiful and a joy to behold, but as it withers, it becomes ugly. From the moment of its blooming, it has already imperceptibly begun to wither. Our incorrect mental approach distorts what we perceive, and desire arises which exaggerates the attractiveness of its object. When those for whom we have felt desire grow old and their youth fades, our desire dies. Often, even before that, when we see them as they are—stripped of the fabrications we have created—our desire for them decreases.

We feel attached to a new piece of clothing, but after we have worn it a while and it has been washed several times, the colour begins to change and we no longer find it so attractive. Our attachment to it subsides. Two things are at work here: where the object of our desire or attachment is concerned, it no longer arouses the same response when it becomes old. Furthermore, when we see things as they actually are, free from our fabrications and projections, even attractive things do not arouse such a strong response. Because desire and attachment initially feel pleasurable, it is hard to see them as faulty, but after a while we inevitably experience the problems they bring.

If the swarm of bees is disturbed, the bees become angry, causing themselves and others harm. Similarly, anger is dangerous to ourselves and others and entails much suffering. The husk that covers the grain symbolizes ignorance. The husk prevents one from seeing the grain of rice. Similarly our conceptions of true existence hide the true nature of our minds from us.

The three poisons, when active, are symbolized by filth. The explanation of this analogy refers specifically to semen and blood. These are unappealing to one who is free from sexual desire whereas someone who is full of desire finds them of great interest. The three poisons in manifest form are antithetical to the mentality of the exalted and are active only in ordinary beings. Their activity obstructs attainment of the path of seeing.

The stage of the imprints of ignorance is represented by the earth, which hides the natural treasure. As long as one cannot see the treasure, one will not be able to profit from it. While we remain unaware of our innate Buddha nature, we will do nothing to uncover it and will not be able to attain the nature body of an enlightened being.

We harbour the disturbing emotions, their seeds and their imprints. While the seeds are present, they will keep producing the disturbing emotions whenever the appropriate conditions arise. The imprints cannot produce the disturbing emotions, but they do give rise to the deceptive appearance of true existence. Hinayana Foe Destroyers and Bodhisattvas on the eighth, ninth and tenth stages have rid themselves of the disturbing emotions and their seeds, but because of misleading appearances they perform uncontaminated physical, verbal and mental activities which result in a body, whose nature is mind.[85] This is a subtle body, resulting from the stage of the imprints of ignorance and from uncontaminated action.

In order to attain enlightenment, we must overcome four demonic forces: that of death, the body, the disturbing emotions and the son of the gods. The last force refers to all kinds of interferences to our spiritual practice.[86] The mental body is a subtle form of the demonic force of the body, and even this must in the end be discarded.

The objects to be eliminated by the Hinayana path of seeing are represented by the seed. As the seedling begins to emerge, it casts off the hull of the seed. The selflessness of persons is directly perceived on the uninterrupted phase of the path of seeing, which is followed by the liberated path when one has finally sloughed off all intellectually formed misconceptions.

What remains are the objects to be eliminated by the path of meditation, which are symbolized by the rags that are left when a piece of clothing is worn out. At this point the disturbing attitudes and emotions have been weakened to such an extent that they no longer have the power to influence the practitioner.

The objects to be eliminated on the first seven Bodhisattva stages are represented by the womb. These include what are referred to as inferior obstructions, namely the remaining vestiges of self-interest. Such self-concern does not arise in a coarse form in exalted Bodhisattvas. If it did, it would entail a degeneration of their spirit of enlightenment. Attainment of the non-conceptual wisdom of the eighth Bodhisattva stage is like the birth of the child from the womb.

Just as the impurity of the womb is left behind, so the stains of the impure Bodhisattva stages are now transcended.

There are four phases of existence: existence at the time of death, existence during the intermediate state, existence during the prior period and existence of birth.[87] The existence during the prior period denotes existence at the moment of birth from the womb, and existence of birth refers to the lifetime following the moment of birth. It is said that in the intermediate state we resemble what we will be at the moment of birth, here referred to as the prior period. This term, which is found in traditional literature, has frequently been misinterpreted to mean that during the intermediate state we resemble what we were in our previous rebirth.

When people talk about seeing ghosts, what they see are not those who have died and who are now in the intermediate state because they no longer bear any resemblance to the people they were. Each of us is surrounded by various non-human beings who are not normally visible. They are very familiar with us and give us protection. Sometimes, when we die, they remain behind near our loved ones and may assume our appearance. Because of their familiarity, they may speak or act like us. It is also possible for us to take a rebirth as a non-human being and to return to a place to which we have been very attached. Such non-human beings belong to the realms of gods, demi-gods or hungry spirits. They can be either benevolent or malevolent.

In Tibet when we had something important to do, we would dress in our good clothes and then make a juniper fire. It was customary to jump over this a few times so that the smoke would drive out anything unclean and make way for that which was clean and pure to enter. "Clean" was not necessarily determined by how recently we had washed our clothes or taken a bath but had to do with our life-force and the beings and energies that surrounded us.

The assertion in the *Essence of Those Thus Gone Sutra* that all living beings have this innate disposition, the essence of enlightenment, has been seen by some as an assertion that there is some truly existent inner essence. This, they maintain, contradicts statements in the Perfection of Wisdom sutras which assert that all things are empty of inherent existence and resemble dreams, magical illusions and mirages.

The two are totally compatible, however, because Buddha nature is not something truly existent. In fact, the clear light nature of the mind allows us to rid ourselves of faults and develop unimagined qualities, which could never happen if the mind were truly existent.

6

Overcoming Obstacles

ৎৡৢৢৢৣঌ

Maitreya's *Sublime Continuum* explains that the presence of Buddha nature in all beings is stressed in order to overcome five faults:

> Discouragement, disparaging inferior living beings,
> Holding the incorrect, denigrating what is correct,
> Excessive attachment to the self—these five faults are
> Mentioned so that all who have them can eliminate them.[88]

The first is to feel overwhelmed by the teachings of the Great Vehicle and to think that we lack the capacity to develop the spirit of enlightenment for the sake of all living beings and that enlightenment itself is far beyond our reach. Drawing our attention to the presence of Buddha nature in all beings prevents such discouragement.

Even if we believe that we have the potential to attain enlightenment, we may look down on those we consider our inferiors and underestimate their potential. This second mistake acts as an obstacle to our working for the good of all living beings. To counteract it, we are told that Buddha nature is present in all living beings as a precious source of all good qualities. Recognizing this enables us to cultivate pure perception.

Once the spirit of enlightenment has been developed, we must engage in the activities of Bodhisattvas, of which the most important is the cultivation of wisdom. Emphasis on the clear light nature of the mind, the innately abiding disposition, counteracts the third fault or mistake, the fabrication of true existence, which is our greatest obstacle.

The fourth mistake is to reject the idea that things are empty of true existence and particularly refers to the mistaken idea that Buddha nature itself has not been free of inherent existence from the very outset. This error may occur because one feels that if things lacked true existence, they would be entirely non-existent and the whole presentation of agents and actions and the working of karma would be compromised. The presence of Buddha nature in all beings is emphasized to counteract the notion that because things are not truly existent they must be non-existent and therefore Buddha nature, too, would have no reality. Thus the statement that Buddha nature is present in all beings establishes the two truths—conventional and ultimate reality—in an undistorted way.

The fifth mistake is excessive attachment to the self, which acts as an obstacle to equalizing and exchanging self and others.[89] Here equalizing self and others means to be as concerned about their happiness and freedom from suffering as we are about our own. When exchanging self and others, we transcend even this by cherishing them more than we do ourselves and by being concerned only with their happiness and freedom from suffering. Self-interest and self-preoccupation stop us from developing love and compassion and from engaging in Bodhisattva activities. Understanding that the self does not have true existence and that Buddha nature is equally present in all beings helps us to overcome this excessive attachment to the self.

The explanation of Buddha nature found in the *Sublime Continuum* is first presented in brief. The extended explanation which follows consists of the ten points which establish the clear light nature of the mind as well as the eighteen analogies and what they illustrate. All of these show that the stains are temporary. The *Sublime Continuum* then states the reasons for explaining that all living beings have Buddha nature.

The mind is never without the potential to be separate from stains and never without the potential to develop good qualities, but that potential needs to be activated. As practitioners of the Buddha's teachings, we can do this by repeatedly and sincerely taking refuge and by performing the seven-part practice, which consists of paying homage, making offerings, acknowledging and purifying wrong-doing, rejoicing in the good we ourselves and others have done, requesting the enlightened ones to turn the wheel of the teachings, requesting them to remain in the world and dedicating the merit we have created to the happiness and freedom from suffering of all living beings.[90] This practice lays the foundation for the growth of good qualities and the decrease of our faults and limitations.

Signs that the disposition for the enlightenment of the lesser vehicle is awakening are that we see the disadvantages of cyclic existence and the benefits of liberation more clearly and that when we think of these things and hear teachings on them, tears come to our eyes and we get goose pimples and feel joyful. The awakening of our Mahayana disposition is marked by the same reactions when we hear the profound and extensive teaching of the Great Vehicle and by the development of great compassion. Just as smoke indicates the presence of fire and mist the presence of water, so these signs indicate the awakening of our disposition for enlightenment.

How should one whose disposition has been awakened be led on to the path? Those with a definite disposition for the Hearer, Solitary Realizer or Mahayana vehicle should be given the teachings pertaining to that vehicle to activate their seed of uncontaminated wisdom. Though, according to the Madhyamika view, there is only one ultimate vehicle and all living beings will eventually attain complete enlightenment, if those with the disposition for the enlightenment of the Lesser Vehicle are taught the paths and stages of the Great Vehicle, it will slow down their progress. They may begin to practise the teachings of the Great Vehicle, but because of their disposition, they will sooner or later revert to the practices of the Lesser Vehicle. If they are allowed to follow their disposition from the outset, they will first attain liberation from cyclic existence and then enter the Mahayana paths. This will be the quickest way for them. All of the Buddha's teachings are equally valuable because they are tailored to different temperaments, inclinations and abilities. Doctors do not make a value judgement when they prescribe one medicine and not another for a particular patient.

Those whose disposition is indefinite and whose direction will be determined by whatever teachings they receive should, if possible, from the outset be given Mahayana teachings as the practice of these will lead directly to highest enlightenment.

Being born in a situation that robs us of the freedom to practise, having weak imprints of virtue, being on a wrong path and having strong disturbing emotions are all obstacles which temporarily prevent the awakening of our disposition for enlightenment.

The benefits of awakening our Mahayana disposition are that our interest and faith in the profound and extensive teachings will grow and become more stable as will our determination to attain enlightenment; our enthusiasm to practise will increase; when we practise, we will do so more energetically and we will not take rebirth in any of the bad states.

Are we Buddha nature? In a manner of speaking we are because we can become Buddhas. We defined Buddha nature as that which has the potential to become the body of a Buddha. Our innately abiding disposition becomes the nature body of a Buddha, and the one who possesses it becomes an exalted Buddha.

Notes

❧❦❧

Abbreviation: P: TIBETAN TRIPITAKA (Tokyo-Kyoto: Tibetan Tripitaka Research Foundation, 1956)

1. The truth body (*chos sku*) of an enlightened being consists of the wisdom truth body (*ye shes chos sku*) and the nature body (*ngo bo nyid sku*). The wisdom truth body results mainly from the great store of insight and embodies complete personal development. It is perceived only by other enlightened beings. The form bodies (*gzugs sku*) result primarily from the great store of merit and consist of the enjoyment (*longs sku*) and emanation bodies (*sprul sku*). These are manifestations of enlightened form for the benefit of others. The enjoyment body teaches continually and is perceived only by exalted beings. Emanation bodies are perceived by all those with the karmic predispositions to do so. The nature body (*ngo bo nyid sku*) of an enlightened being is the reality or emptiness of intrinsic existence of an enlightened being's mind.

2. The conventional spirit of enlightenment (*kun rdzob byang chub kyi sems*) is the consciousness accompanying the intention to become enlightened for the sake of all living beings. The ultimate spirit of enlightenment (*don dam byang chub kyi sems*) is the direct understanding of reality, namely that all phenomena are empty of inherent existence, supported by this intention.

3. The Mahayana disposition (*theg chen gyi rigs*) is also called Buddha nature (*sangs rgyas kyi rigs*). Throughout "disposition" is used to translate the word *rigs*, which is frequently used on its own.

4. When the Buddha Shakyamuni came to our world from the Tushita pure land (dGa' ldan yid dga' chos 'dzin), Maitreya (rJe brtsun Byams pa) took over as its spiritual ruler. He will eventually manifest in this world as the next Buddha and display

the deeds of a supreme emanation body (*mchog gi sprul sku*). It
is said that if one hears and thinks about the five treatises, which
he revealed to the great Indian master Asanga (Thogs med),
one will be reborn in the Tushita pure land. In Tibet many of
the largest statues were of Maitreya who is represented sitting
on a throne with his feet on the ground, ready to rise and come
into the world. Just as Avalokiteshvara is the embodiment of
perfect compassion, Maitreya is the embodiment of perfect love.

His *Ornament for Clear Realization* (*Abhisamayālaṃkāra,
mNgon par rtogs pa'i rgyan*, P5184, Vol.88) is a Mahayana text
containing instructions on the hidden aspects of the Perfection
of Wisdom sutras. The fact that there are twenty-one Indian
commentaries on this work and many others by Tibetan masters
indicates its great importance. Its subject-matter served as the
basis for all the later Tibetan literature on the stages of the path.

Maitreya's *Ornament for the Mahayana Sutras*
(*Mahāyānasūtrālaṃkāra, Theg pa chen po'i mdo sde'i rgyan*,
P5521, Vol.108) describes the Mahayana basis for practice,
which includes the disposition for enlightenment, the Mahayana
paths and the extensive deeds of Bodhisattvas as well as their
fruit. It is a commentary on the extensive deeds aspect of the
Buddha's teachings and presents its subject-matter from the
Chittamatra point of view. It was one of the major texts of the
Kadampa (dKa' gdams pa) school.

His *Sublime Continuum of the Great Vehicle*
(*Mahāyānottaratantraśāstra, Theg pa chen po rgyud bla ma'i bstan
bcos*, P5525, Vol.108) has eight chapters as will be explained later.

His other two treatises are *Differentiating Phenomena and the
Nature of Phenomena* (*Dharmadharmatāvibhaṅga, Chos dang chos
nyid rnam par 'byed pa*, P5523, Vol.108); *Differentiating the
Middle Way and the Extremes* (*Madhyāntavibhaṅga, dBus dang
mtha' rnam par 'byed pa*, P5522, Vol.108).

5.   The five paths are the path of accumulation (*tshogs lam*), the
path of preparation (*sbyor lam*), the path of seeing (*mthong lam*),
the path of meditation (*sgom lam*) and the path of no more
learning (*mi slob lam*). In the Lesser Vehicle these five paths
lead to liberation from cyclic existence. In the Great Vehicle

they lead to complete enlightenment. One enters the Mahayana path of accumulation and becomes a Bodhisattva when the spirit of enlightenment is spontaneously and constantly present. At this point one begins to accumulate the great stores of merit and insight necessary for the attainment of enlightenment. The path of preparation, marked by the union of a calmly abiding mind and special insight focusing on emptiness, prepares one for the direct perception of reality. When this experience of reality is achieved, one becomes an exalted being and attains the path of seeing and the first Bodhisattva stage. On the path of meditation the Mahayana practitioner gains ever-increasing familiarity with the direct perception of emptiness and practises the perfections, eliminating more and more subtle obstructions to enlightenment. When all of these have been removed, one attains the path of no more learning and becomes an enlightened being.

6. Gampopa (sGam po pa, also known as Dvags po lha rje bSod nams rin chen, 1079-1153) was one of the foremost disciples of Milarepa (Mi la ras pa, Thos pa dga' 1040-1123) and the author of the *Wish-fulfilling Jewel of the Excellent Teachings, the Precious Ornament for Liberation* (*Dam chos yid bzhin gyi nor bu thar pa rin po che'i rgyan*), which is a text on the stages of the path to enlightenment.

7. *Mahāparinirvāṇasūtra, Yongs su mya ngan las 'das pa chen po'i mdo*, P789, Vol.31.

8. *Mahāparinirvāṇasūtra, Yongs su mya ngan las 'das pa chen po'i mdo*, P788, Vol.31.

9. The proponents of the four schools of Buddhist philosophical tenets are the Vaibhashikas (Bye brag smra ba), the Sautrantikas (mDo sde pa), the Chittamatrins (Sems tsam pa) and the Madhyamikas (dBu ma pa), consisting of the Svatantrikas (Rang rgyud pa) and the Prasangikas (Thal 'gyur pa). See Sopa and Hopkins, *Cutting Through Apearances: Practice and Theory of Tibetan Buddhism* (Ithaca: Snow Lion Publications, 1989) for a succinct presentation of these systems of thought.

10. Hearers (*snyan thos*) and Solitary Realizers (*rang sangs rgyas*) are

intent on gaining personal liberation. They are practitioners of the Hinayana or Lesser Vehicle (*theg pa dman pa*), so called because their objective is limited to their own ultimate well-being. Practitioners of the Mahayana or Great Vehicle (*theg pa chen po*), which consists of the Perfection Vehicle (*pha rol tu chin pa'i theg pa*) and the Secret Mantra Vehicle (*gsang sngags kyi theg pa*), aspire to attain complete enlightenment (*rdzogs pa'i byang chub*) for the sake of all beings and therefore have a considerably greater objective. The practices of the Lesser Vehicle, however, form the essential foundation for those of the Great Vehicle. Solitary Realizers accumulate more merit over a longer period than Hearers and do not depend upon the instructions of a spiritual teacher in their last rebirth before they attain liberation and become Foe Destroyers (*dgra bcom pa*)—those who have completely destroyed the disturbing emotions and their seeds. Liberation in the Hearer and Solitary Realizer Vehicles is referred to as the enlightenment of these vehicles. Practitioners of both the Lesser Vehicle and the Great Vehicle become exalted beings when they gain direct perception of reality.

11.   The three realms are the desire, form and formless realms (*'dod khams, gzugs khams, gzugs med khams*). The desire realm includes hell-beings, hungry spirits, animals, humans, demi-gods and celestial beings belonging to this realm. There are seventeen abodes within the form realm, rebirth in which results from the practice of meditative stabilization. There are four abodes within the formless realm in which one is born as a result of more subtle states of meditative stabilization and through viewing the form realm as a coarse state and the formless realm as refined and preferable. All these states of rebirth are still within cyclic existence. The three realms sometimes also refer to what is below, on and above the ground.

12.   An ordinary person (*so so skye bo*) is one who has not yet had direct experience of emptiness, the nature of reality. Hearers, Solitary Realizers and Bodhisattvas on the paths of accumulation and preparation are included in this category. All those who have had this experience, which first occurs on the path of seeing,

are classed as exalted beings (*'phag pa*). This includes exalted Buddhas (*sangs rgyas 'phag pa*).

13. *Sutra on the Code of Ethical Discipline* (*Vinayasūtra*, *'Dul ba'i mdo*, P5619, Vol.123) refers to Gunaprabha's (Yon tan 'od) commentary on four of the Buddha's teachings on ethical discipline (*bDul ba lung sde bzhi*) for the ordained: *Vinayavastu*, *bDul ba lung gzhi*, P1030, Vols.41-42; *Vinayavibhaṅga*, *bDul ba rnam 'byed pa*, P1032, Vols.42-43; *Vinayagama*, *bDul ba phran tshegs kyi gzhi*, P1035, Vol.44; *Vinayauttaragrantha*, *bDul ba gzhung dam pa*, P1037, Vol.45.

14. The four features characterizing the disposition of the exalted (*'phags pa'i rigs bzhi*), namely those who have had direct perception of reality, are contentment with poor clothing (*chos gos ngan ngon tsam gyis chok shes pa*), contentment with meager alms (*bsod snyoms ngan ngon tsam gyis chok shes pa*), contentment with a poor dwelling (*gnas mal ngan ngon tsam gyis chok shes pa*), and a liking for getting rid of what needs to be discarded and for meditation (*spong ba dang sgom pa la dga' ba*).

15. Three kinds of faith are described. They are clear faith (*dang ba'i dad pa*), the faith of conviction (*yid ches kyi dad pa*) and aspiring faith (*mngon 'dod kyi dad pa*). The first focuses on the marvellous qualities of an enlightened being with a vivid sense of appreciation which makes our mind bright and clear, dispelling disturbing emotions. Our mind becomes like water in which the mud has settled. The faith of conviction arises when we gain certainty that practice of the paths will yield the promised insights and that we can rid ourselves of all mental stains. Aspiring faith is the strong wish to practise in order to gain these realizations and to rid ourselves of faults.

16. Shantideva (Zhi ba lha) lived in the monastic university of Nalanda during the eighth century. To others he appeared quite unaccomplished, and they said he only knew three things: how to eat, sleep and defecate. In an attempt to humiliate him, he was designated to teach before a large gathering. To everyone's amazement he showed himself to be a very great master by teaching his guide to the Bodhisattva way of life, the *Way of the Bodhisattva* (*Bodhisattvacaryāvatāra*, *Byang chub sems dpa'i spyod*

pa la 'jug pa, P5272, Vol.99), and by displaying miraculous feats. English translations: *A Guide to the Bodhisattva's Way of Life*, Stephen Batchelor, trans. (Dharamsala: Library of Tibetan Works and Archives, 1979); *The Bodhicaryāvatāra*, Kate Crosby and Andrew Skilton, trans. (Oxford: Oxford University Press, 1995); *A Guide to the Bodhisattva Way of Life*, Vesna A. Wallace and B. Alan Wallace, trans. (Ithaca: Snow Lion Publications, 1997); *The Way of the Bodhisattva*, Padmakara Translation Group, trans. (Boston: Shambhala Publications, 1997).

17.   The Indian master Vasubandhu (dByig gnyen) probably lived in the fourth century. He is said to have held the Chittamatra philosophical view, but his *Treasury of Knowledge* (*Abhidharmakośa, Chos mngon pa'i mdzod*, P5590, Vol.115) is written from a Vaibhashika standpoint. It has eight chapters of which the first three deal with the first noble truth, true suffering. The fourth chapter deals with actions as true sources of suffering, and the fifth with the disturbing attitudes and emotions as true sources of suffering. This chapter also discusses true cessations, the third noble truth. The sixth chapter is about true paths, the fourth noble truth, and persons on the paths. The seventh chapter discusses different kinds of awareness, knowledge and extra-sensory perception. The eighth is about various states of absorption.

18.   The seventh Dalai Lama, Gyelwa Kelsang Gyatso (rGyal ba bsKal bzang rgya mtsho) was born in 1708 in Litang (Li thang) in eastern Tibet. He died in 1757.

19.   *zag med sems kyi nus pa*

20.   The followers of scripture (*lung gi rjes 'brangs*) of the Chittamatra school of philosphy are those mainly relying upon the works of the Indian master Asanga while the followers of reasoning (*rigs pa'i rjes 'brangs*) mainly rely upon the works of the Indian masters Dignaga (Phyogs glang) and Dharmakirti (Chos kyi grags pa). The latter posit five kinds of sense consciousness (*dbang shes*) and mental consciousness (*yid shes*) while the former posit eight kinds of consciousness: the five kinds of sense consciousness, mental consciousness, foundational consciousness (*kun gzhi*) and

afflicted mind (*nyon yid*). Afflicted mind mainly consists of misconceptions of the self. Foundational consciousness, which is unobstructed and neutral, carries the imprints of past virtuous and non-virtuous actions.

21. Innately abiding disposition: *rang bzhin gnas rigs*; developmental disposition: *rgyas 'gyur gyi rigs*.

22. The Kadampa (bKa' gdams pa) tradition was founded by Dromtön Gyelway Jungnay ('Brom ston rGyal ba'i byung gnas, 1004-1064), a lay practitioner and the main Tibetan disciple of the Indian master Atisha (982-1054). The Kadampa masters were known for their down-to-earth approach to practice, which they presented according to the three levels of capacity explained in Atisha's *Lamp For The Path to Enlightenment* (*Bodhipathapradīpa, Byang chub lam gyi sgron ma*, P5343, Vol.103). In public they laid great emphasis on the practice of sutra and kept their personal practice of tantra hidden. They regarded all of the Buddha's words (*bka*) as actual instructions (*gdams*) for practice.

23. The Indian master Asanga (Thogs med), who lived in the fourth century, was a trailblazer in establishing the Chittamatra (*sems tsam pa*) system of philosophical tenets although he himself is said to have held the more subtle Prasangika-Madhyamika (*dbu ma thal 'gyur pa*) philosophical view. Asanga wrote five treatises on the different levels of practice. His *Hearer Stages* (*Śrāvakabhūmi, Nyan sa*, P5537, Vol.110) explains the paths of practice of the Lesser Vehicle. His *Bodhisattva Stages* (*Bodhisattvabhūmi, Byang sa*, P5538, Vol.110), which was frequently taught by the Kadampa masters, explains the paths of the Great Vehicle.

24. *Mahāyānottaratantra śāstravyākhyā, Theg pa chen po'i rgyud bla ma'i bstan bcos kyi rnam par bshad pa*, P5526, Vol.108.

25. From Asanga's *Bodhisattva Stages*:
byang chub sems dpa' ni rigs la brten cing gnas nas/ bla na med pa yang dag par rdzogs pa'i byang chub mngon par rdzogs par 'tshangs rgya ba'i skal ba can du 'gyur zhing/ mthu yod par 'gyur ba'i phyir te/ de lta bas na rigs ni skal ba dang ldan pa'i gzhi zhes bya'o

26.   *thos pa'i bag chags*

27.   This is the twelve part process by which we continue to take one
      involuntary rebirth after another and which through stopping
      we can extricate ourselves from cyclic existence. The twelve links
      of dependent arising (*rten 'brel yan lag bcu gnyis*) are normally
      enumerated in the following order: ignorance (*ma rigs pa*),
      formative action (*'du byed*), consciousness (*rnam par shes pa*),
      name and form (*ming gzugs*), the sources (*skyed mched*), contact
      (*reg pa*), feeling (*tshor ba*), craving (*sred pa*), grasping (*len pa*),
      existence (*srid pa*), birth (*skye ba*), ageing and death (*rga shi*).

28.   *yod dang mchog dang mtshan nyid dang*
      rtags dang rigs rab dbye ba dang
      nyes dmigs dang ni phan yon dang
      dpe rnam gnis te rnam pa bzhi

29.   *khams rnams dang ni mos pa dang*
      sgrub pa tha dad dbye ba dang
      'Bras bur tha dad dmigs pa'i phyir
      rigs yod nyid du nges par brjod

30.   *de dge khyad par 'phags pa dang*
      thams cad dang ni don chen dang
      mi zad pa yi rgyu mtshan phyir
      rigs mchog nyid ces brjod pa yin

31.   The ten powers (*stobs bcu*) of an enlightened one are the power
      of knowing what is a cause and what is not a cause for a par-
      ticular result (*gnas dang gnas min mkyen pa'i stobs*); the power of
      knowing the maturation of actions (*las kyi rnam par smin pa
      mkyen pa'i stobs*); the power of knowing different interests (*mos
      pa sna tshogs mkyen pa'i stobs*); the power of knowing different
      dispositions (*khams sna tshogs mkyen pa'i stobs*); the power of
      knowing different faculties (*dbang po sna tshogs mkyen pa'i stobs*);
      the power of knowing the paths to all goals, such as what paths
      lead to a good rebirth, to liberation or to complete enlighten-
      ment, (*thams cad du 'gro ba'i lam mkyen pa'i stobs*); the power of
      knowing what kinds of meditative absorptions rid one of which
      disturbing emotions and the purified results they bring (*kun*

nas nyon mongs pa dang rnam par byang ba mkyen pa'i stobs); the power of knowing past lives (*sngon gyi gnas rjes su dran pa mkyen pa'i stobs*); the power of knowing in what realm of existence death occurred and in what realm birth will occur (*'chi 'pho ba dang skye ba mkyen pa'i stobs*); the power of knowing the end of all contamination (*zag pa zad pa mkyen pa'i stobs*).

The four kinds of fearlessness (*mi 'jigs pa bzhi*) of an enlightened being are fearlessness in asserting that one has eliminated everything that must be eliminated for one's own good (*rang don du spangs pa thams cad spangs zhes dam bcas pa la mi 'jigs pa*), fearlessness in asserting that one possesses all the qualities needed for one's own good (*rang don du yon tan thams cad dang ldan zhes dam bcas pa la mi 'jigs pa*), fearlessness in asserting for the good of others what the counteractive paths are (*gzhan don du gnyen po'i lam 'di dag go dam bcas pa la mi 'jigs pa*) and fearlessness in asserting for the good of others what needs to be eliminated (*gzhan don du 'di dag spang bya yin dam bcas pa la mi 'jigs pa*).

32. The obstructions to liberation (*nyon sgrib*) consist of the disturbing attitudes and emotions and their seeds. The seeds are the potential for them to arise again. The obstructions to knowledge of all phenomena (*shes sgrib*) primarily consist of the imprints left by the disturbing attitudes and emotions.

33. *rang bzhin dang ni rgyas pa dang*
    de ni rten dang brten pa dang
    yod med nyid dang yon tan ni
    sgrol ba'i don du shes par bya

34. The paths of accumulation and preparation are therefore referred to as the stages of belief: *mos pa byas pa'i sa.*

35. *sbyor ba'i sngon du snying rje dang*
    mos pa dang ni bzod pa dang
    dge la yang dag spyod pa ni
    rigs kyi rtags su shes par bya

36. Geshe Chekawa (dGe bshes mChad kha ba, 1101-1175), the author of the *Seven Points For Training The Mind* (*Blo sbyong don bdun ma*), was inspired by Geshe Langritangpa's (dGe bshes

Glang ri thang pa, 1054-1123) words from the *Eight Verses for Training the Mind* (*Blo sbyong tshig brgyad ma*). Both masters belonged to the Kadampa school.

37. The practices of giving (*sbyin pa*), ethical discipline *(tshul khrims)*, patience (*bzod pa*), enthusiastic effort (*brtson 'grus*), concentration (*bsam gtan*) and wisdom (*shes rab*) become perfections and practices of Bodhisattvas when the intention underlying them is the altruistic wish to become enlightened for the sake of all living beings. The first five are said to be like a group of blind people who cannot reach the destination of enlightenment without wisdom, which is like their sighted guide. Concentration and wisdom are more easily practised by ordained people than by lay people. Those who live the life of a householder, however, have plenty of opportunities to practice the first three perfections. Whether lay or ordained it is important to develop enthusiastic effort, which is a delight in virtue.

38. *rigs ni nges dang ma nges dang*
     rken rnams kyis ni mi 'phrogs dang
     'phrogs pa nyid de mdor na rigs
     dbye ba 'di ni rnam pa bzhi

39. *nyon mongs goms dang grogs ngan dang*
     'phongs dang gzhan gyi dbang nyid dang
     mdor na rigs kyi nye dmigs ni
     rnam pa bzhi ru shes par bya

40. *ring mo zhig na ngan song du*
     'gro zhing myur du thar pa dang
     de na'ng sdug bsngal chung ngu myong
     skyo bcas sems can smin par byed

41. *gser gyi rigs bzhin shes par bya*
     dge ba dpag tu med pa'i gnas
     ye shes dang ni dri med ldan
     mthu rnams kyi yang gnas yin no

42. *rin chen mchog rigs bzhin shes bya*
     byang chub chen po'i rgyu mtsan phyir

ye shes che dang ting 'dzin 'phags
sems can mang po'i don gnas phyir

43. *la la gcig tu nyes par spyod nges yod*
la la dkar po'i chos rnams kun tu bcom
la la dkar po'i cha mthun dge ba med
dkar po dman pa yod pa rgyu dang bral

44. The five extremely grave actions (*mtshams med lnga*), which lead straight to a bad rebirth without any intervening (*mtshams med pa*) life, are killing one's mother, father, a Foe Destroyer; causing schism within the spiritual community and drawing blood from the body of a Buddha with the intention to harm. The five almost as grave actions (*nye ba'i mtshams med lnga*), which also lead straight to a bad rebirth, are incest with one's mother if she is a Foe Destroyer, murdering a Bodhisattva, murdering an exalted being of the Lesser Vehicle, stealing what belongs to the spiritual community and destroying a monastery or reliquary monument out of hatred.

45. *de bzhin nyid ni thams cas la*
kyad par med par dag gyur pa
de bzhin gshegs nyid de yi phyir
'gro kun de yi snying po can

46. *Tathāgatagarbhasūtra, De bzhin gshegs pa'i sning po'i mdo*, P 924, Vol. 36

47. *yon tan shin tu rgya che byang chub shing skyed phyir*
bde dang sdug bsngal chen po zhi ba thob bya'i phyir
bdag dang gzhan la phan bde byed pa 'bras bu'i phyir
rigs mchog de ni rtsa ba bsang po lta bu yin.

48. *Dharmadhātustotra, Chos kyi gbyings su bstod pa*, P2010, Vol.46. The Indian master Nagarjuna (Klu sgrub, first to second century) was the trailblazer who established the Madhyamika or Middle Way system of philosophical tenets which propound that while nothing has true existence, the conventional existence of actions and agents is feasible. His most famous work, the *Treatise on the Middle Way (Madhyamakaśāstra, dBu ma'i bstan bcos*, P5224, Vol.95), also called *Fundamental Wisdom (rTsa ba*

shes rab), is a work in twenty-seven chapters which presents the explicit content of the Perfection of Wisdom sutras. Employing a wide variety of approaches and lines of reasoning, it emphasizes dependent arising and explains the paths of insight related to the understanding of emptiness.

49.   *rin chen nam mkha' chu dag bzhin*
      rtag tu rang bzhin nyon mongs med

50.   The reality of the mind with stains: *dri ma dang bcas pa'i sems kyi chos nyid*; the suchness of the mind with stains: *dri ma dang bcas pa'i sems kyi de bzhin nyid*

51.   Sources of the adamantine: *rdo rje'i gnas*

52.   The constituent: *khams*

53.   The seven vajra topics are: the enlightened ones (*sangs rgyas*), the teachings (*chos*), the spiritual community (*dge 'dun*), the constituent, (*khams*) which refers to Buddha nature, enlightenment (*byang chub*), qualities (*yon tan*) and enlightened activity (*phrin las*).

54.   *rdzogs sangs sku'i ni 'phro phyir dang*
      de bzhin nyid dbyer med phyir dang
      rigs yod phyir na lus can kun
      rtags tu sang rgyas snying po can

55.   The essence of Those Thus Gone: *de bzhin gshegs pa'i snying po*; the constituent which is the essence of Those Gone to Bliss: *khams bde bar gshegs pa'i snying po*

56.   High status: *mngon mtho*; definite goodness: *nges legs*

57.   The Indian master Arya Vimuktisena ('Phags pa rNam grol sde) is reputed to have been one of the last disciples of Vasubandhu who lived in the fourth century. He was a great teacher of the Perfection of Wisdom sutras and thousands of fully ordained monks attended his teachings. He became head of twenty-four monasteries in the east of India. His two commentaries on the *Perfection of Wisdom Sutra in Twenty-five Thousand Verses* are generally referred to as *Illuminating the*

Twenty Thousand (Nyi khri snang ba) in Tibetan. They are *Pañ-cavimśatisahasrikā prajñāpāramitopadeśa śāstrābhisamayā-laṃkāravṛtti (Shes rab kyi pha rol tu phyin pa stong phrag nyi shu lnga pa'i men ngag gi bstan bcos mngon par rtogs pa'i rgyan gyi 'grel pa*, P5185, Vol.88) and *Pañcavimśatisahasrikā praj-ñāpāramitopadeśa śāstrābhisamayālaṃkāra kārikāvārtikka (Shes rab kyi pha rol tu phyin pa stong phrag nyi shu lnga pa'i men ngag gi bstan bcos mngon par rtogs pa'i rgyan gyi tshig le'ur byas pa'i rnam par 'grel pa*, P5186, Vol.88).

58. *ngo bo rgyu 'bras las ldan 'jug pa dang*
    gnas skabs de bzhin kun tu 'gros ba'i don
    rtag tu mi 'gyur yon tan dbyer med ni
    don dam dbying kyi gongs don yin zhes bya

59. The final or ultimate stain: *dri ma mthar thug*

60. A wrong cognition: *log shes*

61. *dge slong dag sems la sems ma mchis te sems kyi rang bzhin 'od gsal ba'o*

62. Identity: *ngo bo'i don*

63. Causes: *rgyu'i don*

64. Causes for purifying the suchness of stains and for the development of the disposition to the highest perfection, the truth body: *de bzhin nyid dri mas rnam par dag pa'i gyu dang rigs yongs su sbyangs ba'i chos sku*

65. Suchness with stains: *dri ma dang bcas pa'i de bzhin nyid*

66. The Indian master Chandrakirti (Zla ba grags pa) was one of the main spiritual heirs of Nagarjuna, whose works on sutra and tantra he elucidated and propagated. He lived in the monastic university of Nalanda during the seventh century and was an accomplished practitioner. His *Supplement to the Middle Way (Madhyamakāvatāra, dBu ma la 'jug pa*, P5261, P5262, Vol.98) is a commentary on Nagarjuna's *Treatise on the Middle Way*, which it supplements by explaining the extensive aspect of the path, the practice of skillful means. The subject-matter of the *Supplement* is presented in terms of the ten Bodhisattva

stages. For a translation of the first five chapters, see Jeffrey Hopkins, *Compassion in Tibetan Buddhism* (London: Rider, 1980; rpt. Ithaca: Snow Lion, 1985) and for a translation and extensive explanation of seven verses of the sixth chapter, see Anne Klein, *Path to the Middle* (Albany: State University of New York Press, 1994).

67. Effect: *'bras bu'i don*

68. Gone beyond cleanness, pleasurableness, permanence and selfhood: *gtsang bde rtag dag gi pha rol tu phyin pa*

69. Function: *las kyi don*

70. Possession: *ldan pa'i don*

71. The six different forms of super-knowledge or higher perception are as follows: knowledge of miraculous feats (*rdzu 'phrul gyi mngon shes*) allows Bodhisattvas to reach different worlds in order to find those with whom they have a particularly strong karmic connection. Through knowledge of others' minds (*gshan sems shes pa'i mngon shes*) they are able to discern the different abilities, inclinations, interests and dispositions of those they wish to help, so that what they do will be entirely appropriate. With the divine ear (*lha'i rna ba'i mngon shes*), a form of clairaudience, they can hear what is going on in other worlds and pure lands. Knowledge of past places (*sngon gyi gnas rjes su dran pa'i mngon shes*) permits them to remember the spiritual teachers, people and practices with which they have had a close connection in the past. Knowledge of death and rebirth (*'chi 'pho dang skye ba'i mgon shes*) enables them to know where they and others will be reborn. Knowing the end of contamination (*zag pa zad pa'i mngon shes*) is a personal understanding gained through meditation and higher perception of the paths of practice which lead to liberation and of how to communicate this understanding to others. The end of contamination refers to true cessation (*'gog bden*).

72. The stainless knowledge of the end of contamination: *zag pa zad pa'i ye shes dri med*

73. Stainless elimination: *dri ma med pa'i spang pa*

74. Engagement: *'jug pa'i don*

75. Non-purification of stains: *dri mas ma dag pa*; separation from one aspect: *phyogs gcig dang bral ba*; separation from all obstructions: *sgrib pa thams bcas dang bral ba*

76. Phases: *gnas skabs kyi don*

77. Pervasion: *kun nas 'gro ba'i don*

78. Immutability: *mi 'gyur ba'i don*

79. No differentiation: *dbyer med pa'i don*

80. The stage of the imprints of ignorance: *ma rigs pa'i bag chags kyi sa*

81. The divine eye (*lha'i mig*) is a kind of super-knowledge or clairvoyance.

82. The truth body of realizations: *rtogs pa chos sku*

83. Definitive sutras which explain the ultimate: *don dam ston pa'i nges don gyi mdo*; interpretable sutras which explain the conventional: *kun rdzob ston pa'i drang don gyi mdo*.

84. The seven riches of the exalted (*'phags pa'i nor bdun*) are faith (*dad pa*), ethical discipline (*tshul khrims*), hearing (*thos pa*) meaning extensive knowledge of the teachings, generosity (*gtong ba*), a sense of shame or self-respect (*ngo tsha shes pa*), a sense of embarrassment or decency (*khrel yod pa*) and wisdom (*shes rab*).

85. Mental body: *yid lus*

86. The four demonic forces (*bdud bzhi*) are the demonic force of the lord of death (*'chi bdag gi bdud*), the demonic force of the body (*phung po'i bdud*), the demonic force of the disturbing emotions (*nyon mongs pa'i bdud*) and the demonic force of the son of the gods (*lha'i bu yi bdud*).

87. Existence at the time of death: *'chi srid*; existence during the intermediate state: *bar srid*; existence during the prior period: *mngon dus kyi srid pa*; and existence of birth: *skye srid*.

88. *sems zhum sems can dman la brnyas pa dang*
    yang dag min 'dzin yang dag chos la skur
    bdag chags lhag pa'i skyon lnga gang dag la
    yod pa de dag de spong don du gsungs

89. Equalizing and exchanging self and others (*bdag gzhan mnyam brje*) is the method for developing the spirit of enlightenment which Shantideva explains in his *Way of the Bodhisattva*. The first step is to make others' well-being as important as our own (*bdag gshan mnyam pa*). Then we think extensively about the many faults and disadvantages of self-concern (*rang gces 'dzin gyi skyon sgo du ma nas bsam pa*) and the many benefits of cherishing and developing concern for others (*gzhan gces 'dzin gyi yon tan sgo du ma nas bsam pa*) and why it is appropriate to cherish them (*gces par 'dzin 'os pa'i rgyu mtshan*). This leads to the actual exchange of self and others (*bdag bzhan brje ba'i bsam pa dngos*) through which we totally reverse our former attitudes. Until now we have been primarily concerned with our own well-being, but now we will put others' well-being first. Formerly we have neglected others, and now we will put our own interest last.

90. There are many versions of this seven-part practice (*yan lag bdun pa*). The words are intended to help the practitioner perform the seven activities which create positive energy and purify wrong-doing, the necessary basis for all other practices. Homage or obeisance (*phyag 'tshal ba*) is made to Buddhas, Bodhisattvas and all noble beings who are our inspiration. We then give them actual and imagined gifts (*mchod pa phul ba*), acknowledge our wrong-doing (*bshags pa phul ba*), rejoice (*rjes su yi rang ba*) in our own and others' virtue, request (*bskul ba*) the enlightened ones to teach in order to dispel the darkness of ignorance, supplicate them (*gsol ba 'debs pa*) not to pass away but to remain in the world to which they bring light, and dedicate (*bsngo ba*) our merit in general and specifically that which is created through the performance of this practice to the peace, happiness and complete enlightenment of all living beings.